SOME
INDIAN EVENTS
OF
NEW ENGLAND

*I*T is our intention from time to time to issue a publication which will prove interesting and of historical value to its readers, and we trust we have succeeded in doing so with this brochure. We hope the impression received will be so favorable that the reader will feel that our publications typify the institution which issues them and that the high standard maintained in their appearance and material is characteristic of the banking service we render.

We shall be very happy if the pleasure derived from our booklets induces our friends to think favorably of the State Street Trust Company when the occasion arises for opening a new bank account or renting a safe deposit box at any of our three offices. We also have storage facilities for silverware and other bulky valuables at our Main and Massachusetts Avenue offices.

It may be that some of our readers will be interested in the fact that our Trust Department is qualified by experience to serve effectively as Agent in the handling of investments, as Trustee of living trusts, as Executor and Trustee under wills and in any other recognized trust capacity.

It will be a pleasure to us to furnish detailed information in regard to any of the various services which we render. Our Main Office is at the corner of State and Congress Streets; the Copley Square Office at 581 Boylston Street, and the Massachusetts Avenue Office is at the corner of Massachusetts Avenue and Boylston Street.

ALLAN FORBES,
President, State Street Trust Company

Boston, 1934.

[Member Federal Reserve System]

THE MARCH OF MYLES STANDISH, LED BY HOBOMOK, THE FAITHFUL FRIEND AND GUIDE OF THE PILGRIMS

Hobomok came to Plymouth in July, 1621, and was of great assistance in extending the trade of the English, and in making friends for them among the near-by tribes. He was one of Massasoit's counsellors. Massasoit, with Squanto and Hobomok, without doubt saved the Colony from being annihilated during the first few years of its existence.

Figures ten, in the mist, marched slowly out of the village.
Standish the stalwart it was, with eight of his valorous army,
Led by their Indian guide, by Hobomok, friend of the white men,
Northward marching to quell the sudden revolt of the savage.
Giants they seemed in the mist, or the mighty men of King David;
Giants in heart they were, who believed in God and the Bible,—

Out of the sea rose the sun, and the billows rejoiced at his coming;
Beautiful were his feet on the purple tops of the mountains;
Beautiful on the sails of the *Mayflower* riding at anchor,
Battered and blackened and worn by all the storms of the winter.
Loosely against her masts was hanging and flapping her canvas,
Rent by so many gales, and patched by the hands of the sailors.

LONGFELLOW.

SOME INDIAN EVENTS

OF

NEW ENGLAND

A Collection of INTERESTING INCIDENTS
in the LIVES of the EARLY SETTLERS
of this Country and the Indians
with Reproductions of RARE PRINTS

Compiled by ALLAN FORBES

(See description on next page)

PRINTED FOR THE

STATE STREET TRUST COMPANY

OF BOSTON

1934

The vignette
on the title-page
has been photographed, by
the kindness of Julius H. Tuttle,
from the Indian weather vane which graced
the cupola of the Old Province House during the
residence of several Colonial governors. The Province
House was known for one hundred years or more as the
home of the Colonial governors and formerly stood on Province Street.
This crude Indian weather vane was presented to the Massa-
chusetts Historical Society by the late Dr. John C.
Warren, father of the late Dr. John Collins
Warren. It was made by Shem Drowne,
who also turned out the famous
grasshopper vane that for
many years adorned
Faneuil Hall.

Arranged and printed by direction of
Walton Advertising & Printing Co.
Boston, Mass.

printed in u. s. a.

FOREWORD

IN selecting the subject for our brochure this year, we have chosen "Some Indian Events of New England." In our long research preparatory to compiling these chapters we have been surprised to find so much authentic material, some of which is derived from contemporary reports and accounts written by Governor Bradford in his diary entitled "Plimouth Plantation" which was presented to Massachusetts by England; from "Mourt's Relation," supposed to contain articles by Bradford, Winslow, Robinson and Cushman, all of the Plymouth Colony; from Winslow in his "Good Newes"; from Governor Winthrop in his interesting diary; and from other later writers of New England History.

The inhabitants of our country have been through many difficult times in the past few hundred years, and especially today our people should recall the critical situations that confronted the Pilgrims and the Puritans when they first arrived and never knew when they might be completely annihilated. We should derive inspiration from the tenacious spirit of the early settlers, which carried them successfully through tremendous trials and hardships. Often the previous owners of the land could have exterminated the Colonists in one fierce attack, but they were probably unaware of their superior strength. Moreover, the friendship of Massasoit and the scourge that decimated the Massachusetts tribe of Indians enabled the newcomers to survive in spite of many hardships.

In studying the information that has been handed down, it becomes at once apparent that the Colonists usually kept accurate records of events, but that the Indian, not knowing how to write, has been unable in most cases to pass down to future generations the problems that confronted his race when the "palefaces" first began to land on our New England shores. Nor has he, for this reason, been able to explain his version of any particular incident. As Professor Warren K. Moorehead, a learned student of the Indian question, makes clear, "the Indian point of view concerning encroachments of white people upon their ancient lands has not been set forth." The aborigines were faced with two courses that they could pursue: either they must subdue the newcomers and hold the territory for their children, or else they must allow the whites to settle peacefully on lands they had possessed for generations. Some leaders chose one policy and some another; but the wiser heads foresaw that they were destined to be overwhelmed eventually by the increasing numbers from across the waters. Massasoit, the best friend of the Plymouth Colony among the redskins, adopted the policy of establishing peace with the English; but his son, the warlike King Philip, chose the aggressive policy which ended in the almost complete annihilation of his race on New England

soil. Two great chieftains foresaw the doom of their tribes, for they expressed themselves very clearly on this point. The Narragansett chief, Miantonomo, made this speech before some of his men: "Brothers, we must be one as the English are, or we shall soon all be destroyed. You know our fathers had plenty of deer and skins, and our plains were full of deer and of turkeys, and our coves and rivers were full of fish. But, brothers, since these English have seized upon our country, they cut down the grass with scythes, and the trees with axes. Their cows and horses eat up the grass and their hogs spoil our beds of clams; and finally we shall starve to death! Therefore, stand not in your own light, I beseech you, but resolve with us to act like men. All the sachems both to the east and west have joined with us, and we are all resolved to fall upon them, at a day appointed, and therefore I have come secretly to you, because you can persuade the Indians to do what you will." Another chief, called Passaconaway, from Pawtucket Falls, on the Merrimack River, upon handing over his authority to his son Wonalancet, is reported to have made this farewell address: "Hearken to the words of your father! I am an old oak that has withstood the storms of more than a hundred winters. Leaves and branches have been stripped from me by the winds. My eyes are dim; my limbs totter; I must soon fall. When young, no one could bury the hatchet in the sapling before me. My arrows could pierce the deer at a hundred rods. No wigwam had so many furs, no pole had so many scalp-locks as Passaconaway's. Then I delighted in war. The whoop of the Pennacooks was heard on the Mohawk, and no voice as loud as Passaconaway's. The scalps upon the pole in my wigwam told the story of Mohawk suffering. The English came; they seized the lands; they followed upon my footpaths. I made war upon them, but they fought with fire and thunder. My young men were swept down before me when no one was near them. I tried sorcery against them but they still increased, and prevailed over me and mine. I, who can take the rattlesnake in my palm as I would a worm without harm—I, that have had communication with the Great Spirit, dreaming and awake—I am powerless before the palefaces. These meadows they shall turn with the plow; these forests shall fall by the axe; the palefaces shall live upon your hunting grounds and make their villages upon your fishing places. The Great Spirit says this and it must be so. We are few and powerless before them. We must bend before the storm. Peace with the white men is the command of the Great Spirit and the wish—the last wish—of Passaconaway."

"All students of these troublesome times," declares Professor Moorehead, "agree that it was necessary for the Indian to be displaced by the superior civilization." It would have been an impossibility for the two races to have lived together harmoniously, although Alvin G. Weeks, in his "Massasoit," expresses the opinion that that policy should have been attempted. "I would turn aside," he says, "to look upon Sachem's Plain and Mount Hope with a feeling of regret that the men who fell there could not have devoted their God-given energy to the accomplishment of their dreams of living with their white

brethren in peace and harmony. A race that could produce a Massasoit is not all bad, and it is a misfortune to the world that the good that was in it could not have developed side by side with the good that our fathers had inherited from the memories of a thousand years of upward struggling towards the light."

There were many great men and women in their way among the Indians, such as Massasoit, Samoset, Squanto, Hobomok, Canonicus, King Philip, Weetamoe, Awashonks, Ninigret, Canonchet, Miantonomo, Chickatabot and others, who undoubtedly stood out in their way as many of our citizens do today.

Most persons think of the Indians as indulging continually in warfare, massacres, pillaging, scalping and burning; but after reading several hundred books relating to the New England aborigines, it is very conclusive that although there was much fighting and brutality on both sides, there were many incidents of the opposite nature, such as treaties carefully observed, kindnesses shown, and captives well treated by both whites and redskins. We have endeavored to narrate the most interesting events connected with the lives of the Colonists and the natives of New England, and we trust that our readers will realize that it is not our desire to glorify the Indian, but to bring more clearly to the public his better qualities. We have gone to great pains to procure pictures of interest and have been successful in finding a good many rare prints of events and of Indians; some were found in the New England States and a few especially attractive ones were discovered in London by Richard Holworthy, who has assisted the State Street Trust Company in compiling the chapter entitled "American Indians in London." To him the Trust Company is much indebted. In this chapter is included an account of Samson Occum and his work in behalf of Dartmouth College, which we believe to be very complete and which should be of especial interest to Dartmouth alumni. The photograph of Occum's house, we understand, has never before been reproduced. There may be some discrepancies in dates and possibly in a few facts, but it must be remembered that even the best historians differ occasionally concerning some of these early events in our history.

We wish to thank particularly J. W. Haley of Providence, a great student of Rhode Island history, for correcting certain paragraphs which refer to events that took place within that state. Professor Warren K. Moorehead, already referred to, made some valuable suggestions to us concerning the subject matter to be dealt with; Chauncey C. Nash was kind enough to mention his name to us originally. As in the past, Howard M. Chapin of the Rhode Island Historical Society has been of assistance in advising us in a number of ways; and another Rhode Island man, R. F. Haffenreffer, owner of the beautiful estate of Mount Hope in Bristol, Rhode Island, one of the haunts of King Philip and the scene of his death, has furnished from his interesting Indian Museum a number of pictures of rare Indian articles for our use. George G. Heye, Director of the Museum of the American Indian in New York City, has also contributed valuable assistance. The Trust Company wishes especially to thank Pierce

E. Buckley, and other officials and members of the staff of the Boston Public Library, for much time and thought given to the selection of particular books and material during three years of research.

Those who have helped us on special chapters and to whom the Trust Company gives much credit are Theodore P. Adams, Robert W. Barclay, J. Robert Bentley, Clarence S. Brigham of the American Antiquarian Society, S. H. Batchelder, Frank Roe Batchelder, Percy W. Brown, David I. Bushnell, William B. Cabot, William H. Claflin, John C. L. Clark, Honorable Frederic W. Cook, Secretary of the Commonwealth, Frederic H. Curtiss of the Federal Reserve Bank of Boston, John Daniels of the English-Speaking Union, George H. Delano, Halsey C. Edgerton, Treasurer of Dartmouth College, Miss J. L. Farnum of the Library of Congress, Otto Fleischner, C. T. Flower, Douglas S. Freeman, Thomas B. Gay, Edward F. Gray, Former British Consul General in Boston, John Hatton, William R. Herlihy, Jr., Alfred E. Johns of the English-Speaking Union in London, Miss Helena Mills John, the late Benjamin N. Johnson, Jerome A. Johnson, Professor Eric P. Kelley, Charles R. Lingley, the late Percival Hall Lombard, H. M. Lydenberg of the New York Public Library, William P. Long, Miss Ruth Gaines of the Huntington Free Library, New York, Robert W. MacMillan, Wyatt Malcolm of the National Museum of Canada, Alva G. Maxwell, Honorable Herbert Parker, Arthur L. Peale, Arthur S. Phillips, Raymond J. Queenin, Professor Leon B. Richardson, Ernest E. Rogers, Henry W. Royal, Curator of Pilgrim Hall, Harold G. Rugg, Professor W. O. Sawtelle, Roger L. Scaife, Harry Worcester Smith, Charles Stewart, Captain F. G. Storr of the Bath and West and Southern Counties Society, England, Mrs. Nathaniel Thayer, George H. Tripp, Julius H. Tuttle, Joseph A. Wallace, Walter R. Whiting, Dr. R. H. Wilds and Bertram Winthrop.

A number of persons, whom we also wish to thank, have assisted the Trust Company in connection with other chapters which we expect will appear in a later booklet, in which suitable acknowledgment will be made.

The Trust Company also wishes to acknowledge the untiring efforts of Miss Katherine G. Rogers, who with the effective assistance of Miss Caroline E. Mayes, has for several years taken care of a large volume of material, so necessary in the preparation of this booklet. The author wishes also to record the careful correction of these chapters by his able Secretary and Vice-President of the Company, Ralph M. Eastman.

To Perry Walton and his staff was entrusted, as usual, the task of arranging and printing the booklet.

We hope that this visit to the hunting grounds and trails of the redmen will be enjoyed by the depositors and friends of the State Street Trust Company.

ALLAN FORBES,
President.

Boston, 1934.

TABLE OF CONTENTS

Courtesy of Massachusetts Historical Society

MASSACHUSETTS BAY COLONY SEAL

The charter granted by Charles I of England to the Governor and Company of the Massachusetts Bay in New England provided that they might have "one comon seale." The seal adopted, of which the above is a reproduction, bore the figure of an Indian uttering the words "Come over and help us," but there is grave doubt that any Indian ever expressed such a sentiment. This seal disappeared some two hundred years ago, the earliest impression from it now known appearing on a document of 1676.

From a photograph by Blackington Service   *Permission of Blackington Service*

STATUE OF MASSASOIT ON COLE'S HILL, PLYMOUTH, MASSACHUSETTS, SHOWING
PLYMOUTH HARBOUR AND THE CANOPY OVER PLYMOUTH ROCK

Massasoit was the Great Sachem of the Wampanoags and was "Protector and Preserver of the
Pilgrims," as the tablet records. He is depicted bearing his peace pipe to the English. He kept a
continuous truce with the Colonists for forty years—from 1621, when he made a treaty, until his
death in 1661. His favorite camp was at Sowams, now part of Warren, Rhode Island. This statue
was erected in 1926 by the Improved Society of Red Men "as a grateful tribute," subscriptions being
received from every state in the Union. The statue is by Cyrus E. Dallin.

Some

INDIAN EVENTS
of NEW ENGLAND

INDIAN ANECDOTES

I N reading many books on the subject of Indians, a number of stories were found which seemed sufficiently amusing or interesting to place together in one chapter. We hear of the many hardships suffered by the Pilgrims, but a few diverting episodes have come to our attention. There is, however, one authentic incident which happened near Plymouth a few days after their landing, and which is well told, probably by Edward Winslow, in one of the chapters in "Mourt's Relation," a work published by George Morton, containing accounts of the first few years in the lives of these colonists.

The Indians were very clever in catching both fish and game. Some of the newcomers wandered a considerable distance from their village and in returning "were shrewdly puzzled," and lost their way. "As we wandered, we came to a tree, where a young sprit was bowed down over a bow, and some acorns strewed underneath. Stephen Hopkins said, it had been to catch some deer. So, as we were looking at it, William Bradford being in the rear, when he came looking also upon it, and as he went about, it gave a sudden jerk up, and he was immediately caught up by the legs. It was a very pretty device, made with a rope of their own making, (of bark or some kind of roots probably,) and having a noose as artificially made as any roper in England can make, and as like ours as can be; which we brought away with us." Some years later when animals had been imported, a horse, in a similar manner, was caught in a trap and suspended in mid-air. Presently an Indian came running into camp and told the English that their "squaw" horse was hanging on a tree.

The aborigines attached great weight to dreams, and several writers have mentioned instances in which advantage was taken of their superstitious ideas. An Indian believed that if he dreamt about a certain incident or event, it became necessary for any such fact or transaction to be at once consummated. In a certain village some redskins were accustomed to call upon a colonist called Johnson, declaring that they had had a dream that he had given them a great deal of rum and tobacco. Johnson, it is related, thought it good policy to appease them by a gift of their favorite concoction. The visits became so frequent that finally the newcomer conceived the bright idea of returning the call, telling his recent guests that he, too, had had a dream that in return for so much hospitality, they had granted him a large tract of land near by. "Have you really dreamt that?" they exclaimed, with a look of despair. A council was thereupon held, and the Indians

with much disappointment on their countenances returned and said, "Brother Johnson, we give you the tract of land—but promise never to dream any more."

Another similar anecdote is related of Sir William Johnson, an Irishman, Mohawk War Chief, and a superintendent of Indian affairs in this country, and old Hendrik, born a Mohegan and later king of one of the six Nations of Mohawks. The Indian "dreamt" for a new English suit of clothes and promptly received it. Sir William a short time later declared that he had had a dream that five thousand acres of land along the Mohawk Valley had been presented to him by his friend. It is said that Hendrik promptly deeded the property, remarking at the same time, "Now, Sir, I will never dream with you again— you dream too hard for me." When Johnson resigned, the Mohawk chief at a conference referred to him as a tree that had grown for their use, and said that he "has large Ears and heareth a gret deal, and what he hears he tells to us; he also has Large Eyes and sees a gret way, and conceals nothing from us." The figures of these two men stand on a pedestal at Lake George, where together they won a battle, although Hendrik lost his life in the encounter. Hendrik, using his long Indian name, was one of the five chiefs to go to London on a mission in 1710, as mentioned later on, and his portrait is later reproduced. There are also several engravings of him in the New York Public Library, one of which is reproduced.

It was quite natural that the Indians should consider they were superior to the whites, for they never had known any race of men other than themselves. A white man once met an Indian and accosted him as "brother," which evidently irritated the latter to such an extent that he begged to be informed how this relationship existed. "By way of Adam," said the colonist, to which the Indian quickly replied, "Me thank him Great Spirit we no nearer brothers." The first sachem of the Narragansetts, Tashtassuck, went further than this, for he was of the opinion that there were no other children among the New England tribes worthy of marrying either his son or his daughter, and so he therefore made them marry each other.

There are several war stories worthy of repetition. A short time before King Philip's War, the Governor of Massachusetts sent an ambassador to Philip to ask him to make a treaty with the people of this Colony, urging him at the same time not to wage war against them. This was the reply received: "Your governor is but a subject of King Charles of England. I shall not treat with a subject. I shall treat of peace only with the king, my brother. When he comes, I am ready." Another Sagamore gave this advice to the chief of another tribe: "You must give no more wampum to the English, for they are no sachems, nor none of their children shall be in their place if they die. They have no tribute given them. There is but one king in England, who is over them all, and if you should send him 100,000 fathom of wampum, he would not give you a knife for it, nor thank you." Canonchet, chief sachem of the Narragansetts, and son of Miantonomo, had just defeated Captain Pierce and his colleagues. During this conflict one of the English, probably the only one to escape, was saved by a clever trick. A Narragansett ally of the colonists started, with raised tomahawk, to pursue this white man,

and the enemy was content to let the redskin continue his chase, as they felt sure he would be able to attain his end unaided. Consequently, both escaped h o m e through the woods.

During this same battle a friendly Christian Indian was pursued by one of Canonchet's men, and as he was losing ground he jumped behind a rock. He believed certain death awaited him, but fortunately he thought of a bit of strategy that doubtless was often attempted in the World War. He raised his cap over the edge of the rock by means of his gun, as if he were trying to sight his enemy. This produced the desired result, for his antagonist shot at the empty cap and, before he could reload, the smarter Indian rushed out from behind the rock and dispatched him quite easily.

Another of Captain Pierce's Indian allies continued to fight until few on his side remained

From "Johnson of the Mohawks," by Arthur Pound
Permission of The Macmillan Company, Publishers

STATUE OF HENDRIK AND
SIR WILLIAM JOHNSON

Overlooking the battlefield at Lake George, where Hendrik was killed and where Sir William, in command of the English troops in North America, won a victory. Hendrik was a sachem of the Mohawks and visited London in 1710 under his Indian name of Etow Oh Kaom, as narrated in this brochure. Of this Indian chief many stories have come down to us.

alive. Looking about him, he quickly noticed that most of the enemy had blackened their faces with powder, whereupon he did the same and managed to escape. This story serves as a reminder of another powder story that has been handed down to us from Indian days. A white trader sold a quantity of this article to a redskin and told him if he sowed it in the ground it would grow like grain, or wheat. The purchaser immediately conceived the idea of growing a quantity of it and getting very rich thereby. When spring approached he planted the powder and then waited patiently for some months to see it appear. Winter came and nothing sprouted. He now began to realize he had been duped. Some time later he obtained a large credit from the same trader for some goods he purchased, and then allowed a long time to elapse without making payment. The Indian's day came shortly. The creditor came for his money, whereupon the redskin, looking him straight in the eye, said, "Me pay you when my powder grow." "The guilty white man," wrote Drake in his "Biography and History of the Indians of North America," "quickly retraced his steps, satisfied, we apprehend, to balance his account with the chagrin he had received."

One Andrew Robinson of Gloucester was captured one day by the Indians, but succeeded in escaping to his sloop, which was three miles away. The Indians, however, chased him and finally caught up with his vessel. Luckily, he happened to remember that he had on board a large quantity of scupper nails which had sharp points and flat heads, and these he strewed broadcast on the deck. The Indians, of course,

were unable to walk, but with his thick soles he was able to do so, and succeeded in knocking them on the head just after they came over the gunwale. This wily Captain was believed to have had a charmed life and a particular talent for killing Indians.

Reverend John Eliot was instrumental in Christianizing many of the Indians, and therefore kept most of them from opposing the colonists in King Philip's War. He had much difficulty, though, in converting Wonalancet, sachem of Pawtucket Falls on the Merrimack River. Although friendly to the English, he refused repeatedly to adopt their religion. Finally, at an advanced age, he adopted Christianity and is reported to have said at that time: "I must acknowledge I have all my days been used to pass in an old canoe, and now you exhort me to change and leave my old canoe and embark in a new one, to which I have hitherto been unwilling, but now I yield up myself to your advice, and enter into a new canoe, and do engage to pray to God hereafter."

It is well known that the settlers at an early date imported liquor, some of which they sold occasionally to the Indians, in spite of drastic laws to prevent it. In some cases deception was practiced and the colonists watered it, believing that they would never be detected. The Indians, however, began to realize that their drinks were growing less strong and adopted the scheme of throwing a little on the fire; if it burned it was of the proper strength and good enough to purchase, but if the reduced article extinguished the fire and would not flame up, it was too weak for them. In this way the expression "fire-water" came to be applied. Several "fire-water" stories are extant. An Indian once was criticized by a white person for something he had done wrong. The chief of the tribe heard of the incident and amusingly remarked: "Send your fire-water to prison, punish *it,* but not those whom it causes to do wrong." A story is told of a sachem who explained in court the bad conduct of a compatriot by punctuating his long speech with empty bottles, thereby affording much amusement. Another redskin who had experienced the ill effects of "fire-water" gave this description of it: "It could only have been distilled from the hearts of wild cats and the tongues of women, it makes me feel so weak and foolish."

There is still another story along the same lines. An influential Nevada Indian called Johnson Sides realized the dangers of drink among his compatriots, and, practicing temperance himself, he advised them always against indulging in any liquor. He often used to say: "My friends, I think whiskey no good, but very bad. Mebbe you take a drink it no much bad, but you take two drinks you kill somebody. Mebbe you want more, you hurt your brother or you lickem squaw, or you burn down a wickiup." One day he was caught drinking a glass of whiskey, was fined, and the papers made fun of this "fallen reformer," all of which injured his feelings very much. In his plight he appealed to one of the Nevada senators, who actually passed this bill: "*Resolved,* By the Senate, the people of the State of Nevada concurring, That the drink of whiskey taken by Johnson Sides on the 17th day of September, in Virginia City, county of Storey, be and is hereby declared null and void." This act seemed to satisfy him, and he continued his temperance lectures.

Another tale is related of an Ottaway chief who was addicted to drink. When asked one day what he believed brandy to be made of, he replied that it was composed of "hearts and tongues." "For," he added, "when I have drunken plentifully of it, my heart is a thousand strong, and I can talk, too, with astonishing freedom and rapidity." It was reported that a redskin was found frozen to death, and his country-men determined to hold an inquest to determine the cause of his demise. Their curiously expressed verdict was said to be, "Death from the freezing of a great quantity of water inside of him," which they were of the opinion he had "drunken for rum." There is still another anecdote apropos of this subject which may bear repetition. In the Connecticut River is a narrow and rocky place, and it is said that only one person ever succeeded in passing this point, and that one person was an Indian woman. She was attempting to cross the river above these rapids in her canoe, which was suddenly swept down stream by the torrent. She realized she was going to almost certain destruction. She had with her a bottle of rum and, seeing it, she promptly raised it to her mouth and never removed it until the last drop had been quaffed. She was picked up below the narrows, lying in the bottom of her canoe, thoroughly intoxicated. When she became sober she was asked why she had drunk so much, with the prospect of death ahead of her; she answered that she realized it was too much, but she couldn't think of allowing any of it to be lost, happen to her what might.

There is a story that shows the conscientiousness of an Indian hus-band. There was a famine in some western town and his wife expressed the desire for some corn. Not having any, he set off on horse-back in search of some. After riding a hundred miles or so, he found enough to fill his hat. It was necessary, however, to give his horse in exchange, and he then walked home with the food, carrying the saddle and bridle with him.

The Indian women per-formed most of the drudgery. An Indian hus-b a n d , upon being asked the reason, replied that it was cus-tomary for the man to go first, carrying his dig-nity, and for the woman to f o l l o w him, carrying every-thing else.

From "Indian Nullification of the Constitutional Laws of Massachusetts, Rela-tive to the Mashpee Tribe; or the Pretended Riot Explained," by William Apes Kindness of the late Percival H. Lombard

SATIRE ON THE MANNER OF INSTRUCTING
THE INDIANS IN EARLY COLONIAL DAYS

At their meals the Indians usually made use of no spoons, or else large spoons, and they laughed at the English for using such small ones, declaring that they had to carry them so often to their mouths that their arms must grow tired much sooner than their stomachs, which was not right.

Another story is connected with Governor Jenks of Rhode Island. During a period of troublesome times he requested an Indian to inform him should any strange redskin visit his wigwam, and promised him a mug of flip for the information. Some time later the Indian called on the magistrate, and this conversation, taken from Drake's book, ensued: "Well, Mr. Guvenor, strange Indian come to my house last night!" "Ah," said the governor, "and what did he say?" "He no speak," replied the Indian. "What, didn't he say anything at all?" added Mr. Jenks. "No, he no speak at all." "That certainly looks suspicious," said his Excellency, and inquired if he were still there; being told that he was, he ordered the promised mug of flip. The visitor finished the drink and, as he was about to depart, remarked, "Mr. Guvenor, my squaw have papoose last night."

One of New York's Governors had a council meeting with the Senecas, and they got into an argument as to the wording of an old treaty. The Governor knew he was right, as he had it written on paper. Red Jacket of the Senecas replied: "The paper then tells a lie; I have it written here," pointing to his brow. "You Yankees are born with a feather between your fingers; but your paper does not speak the truth. The Indian keeps his knowledge here—this is the book the Great Spirit gave us—it does not lie!" The treaty was reread and it was found that the Indian was correct.

The leading magistrate of Massachusetts, Governor Dudley, is mentioned in an anecdote told at the time of building a house on his plantation. He noticed a stalwart Indian watching it progress and asked him if he didn't want to work in order to buy clothes, as it was a cold day and he had little to cover him. "And why you no work, Guvenor?" said the Indian. Dudley, pointing to his forehead, replied that he worked with his head and not with his hands. The redskin then said he would be willing to work, too, and it was agreed that if he would kill a calf he would be paid a shilling. This the Indian proceeded to do. He also dressed it, so the story goes, for another shilling, and then went into a near-by tavern, returning soon to the Governor with the statement that one shilling was a counterfeit. This complaint was repeated, whereupon Dudley was now positive of his roguery, and determined to punish him. He gave the offender a letter directed to the keeper of the prison in Boston, requesting that the bearer be soundly whipped upon arrival. Soon after leaving, the Indian met by chance another Indian who was in the employ of the Governor, and informed him that his master wished him to carry the letter to Boston. Of course the innocent victim received a good thrashing when he reached his destination. Some time later on, Dudley met the tricky Indian and asked him how he dared act so disgracefully. Pointing his finger to his forehead, as the Governor had done some time before, he replied, "Head work, Guvenor, head work."

Walter R. Whiting, who has often given us ideas for our booklets, tells us that his grandmother Cate in Barrington, New Hampshire,

used to tell the Whiting family the anecdotes of the Indian days related to her by her grandparents. One cold evening a shadow was seen to slip across the window, and Mrs. Cate at once realized it was the form of an Indian who had doubtless come to reconnoitre. Her husband had gone to town for some supplies, but she woke the children and determined to make as brave a showing as possible. We will let the Whiting family tell the story in their own words.

"As it was hopeless for them to try to defend their home by force against the odds they faced, their last resort lay in trickery. Quickly she gave directions and the children scattered to their tasks. In a few moments the tread of armed men resounded through the house as they marched to their positions, the floors shook as they rammed home the charge in their muskets and here and there a shutter half opened cautiously as the sentries took their posts while gruff voices called the roll of the many defenders of this lonely farm.

"All night long this army which had sprung as if by magic to Grandma Cate's assistance stood to arms in ceaseless vigil. At intervals the heavy tramp of feet sounded on the stairs, voices called to one another, and lights passed from room to room as the guard was changed. All night long a weary woman and her son knelt at the window, watching the silent fields, knowing that along the edge of the wood keen eyes were on the house, waiting perhaps for the guard to relax its vigil so that the attack might be pressed home. All night long they watched, and when sleep seemed to be overwhelming, they then would take the heavy cheeses which had been piled away for the winter and roll them down the stairs, creating a fearful din as if an army of giants was stamping about the house. In deep voices they would call to the younger children, who pounded on the floor with pots and pans in answer until whole companies had answered to the roll and charged their muskets anew, so that the Indians might know that fresh sentries were on guard against them. Just as morning dawned the son slipped from the house into the forest; with anxious heart Grandma Cate waited until the day had come and he returned with the news that the Indians had gone."

At another time Mrs. Cate looked up and saw two Indians standing by the fireplace. Occasionally a redskin used to drop in on a cold night and wrap himself up in a blanket before the fire, but these visitors were of a different tribe and she was much worried. Again we will copy the words of the narrator. " 'Food!' they grunted and patted their stomachs. She looked at them in concern. There was nothing ready in the house, and she must feed them and get them away; for if her husband should return he might shoot and ask questions later. She knew there must be a large party somewhere near, who would be only too glad to open hostilities. She went to the brick oven, but the brown bread cooking there was still a soggy mess. In desperation she drew it out, dumping it into two large wooden bowls and cooling it with a pan of milk she had set aside to separate. Eagerly the braves took them from her and drank down the heavy gruel, smacking their lips at this strange and delicious food. Three bowls apiece they drank until the brown bread was gone. They explained that the village was to be attacked that evening, but her home would be saved provided she did not warn her neighbors. The Indians departed. Of course

the Cates at once spread the news and the villagers flocked to the garrison house. Grandma Cate herself walked a long way to a farm to give the unwelcome news and on the way back her path was cut off by the Indians. She reached the stockade with much difficulty. When the enemy had finished their pillaging, the Cates visited their farm, expecting, of course, to find the house burned as a revenge for the spreading of the alarm. The Indians, however, had kept their promise, nothing had been touched, and the cattle were grazing peacefully in the fields. It was many years before the war whoop faded from those woods forever, but though farms about it were raided and burned, Grandmother Cate's house stood unmolested, a silent testimony to the red man's word."

There is a rather amusing anecdote that comes from the West. About the year 1794 an American officer presented to a chief a medal, on one side of which was a likeness of George Washington, then President, with a sword in his hand, and on the other side was an Indian depicted as burying his hatchet. The Chieftain looked at it carefully and made the bright remark, "Why does not the President bury his sword too?"

When William Penn visited Charles II he surprised the English monarch by suggesting a purchase of lands from the aborigines. "Buy their lands!" he exclaimed. "Why, is not the whole land mine?" "No, your Majesty," Penn is supposed to have replied. "We have no right to their lands; they are the original occupants of the soil." "What! have I not the right of discovery?" asked the King. "Well," interposed Penn, "just suppose that a canoe full of savages should by some accident discover Great Britain, would you vacate or sell?" Another anecdote along the same lines appears in a pamphlet written by Roger Williams to Governor Bradford against the validity of the colonial charter. "Why lay such stress upon your patent from King James? 'Tis but idle parchment; James has no more right to give away or sell Massasoit's lands, and cut and carve his country, than Massasoit has to sell James's kingdom or to send his Indians to colonize Warwickshire."

The last story we have to offer here is supposed to have taken place in Plymouth and may or may not be true. Hubbard mentions it and Captain Nathaniel Uring, an Englishman who evidently visited most of the ports in the world, and who made a voyage from London to Boston in 1709, wrote that Governor Dudley had narrated this same story, supposing it to be true. "It happened one Day," so wrote Captain Uring, "as the Carpenter was cutting down a large Timber Tree for the Use of the Fort, that great Numbers of Indians stood around it, gazing and admiring the wonderful Dexterity of the Carpenter, and greatly surprised at the Manner of Cutting it, having before the Arrival of the Europeans never seen an Ax, or any such like Tools. The Carpenter perceiving the Tree ready to fall, gave Notice to the Indians by Language, or Signs to keep out of its Reach when it fell; but either for want of understanding the Carpenter, or by Carelessness of the Indians, a Branch of the Tree in its Fall struck one of them and killed him; upon which they raised a great Cry. The Carpenter seeing them much out of Humour at the Accident, made

his Escape into the Fort." The Indians insisted that the carpenter should be killed and the situation looked very serious. The English tried their best to explain that it was the fault of the Indian, but to no purpose. Presents even were of no avail. They then discussed another way of giving them satisfaction, for their numbers were superior to the colonists.

Uring's story continues: "The Carpenter being a useful Man, they considered they could not spare him, without the greatest Inconvenience; but seeing there was an absolute Necessity of doing something, they found out an Expedient which was this: There was in the Fort an old Weaver, who had been Bed-rid a long Time; they concluded to hang up the Weaver, and make the Indians believe it was the Carpenter." They approached the Indians and informed them, according to the narrative, that they desired to please them, "That in the Morning they should see the Carpenter hanging upon such a Tree in their View. In the night they carried the poor old Weaver, and hanged him in the Room of the Carpenter." This gave complete satisfaction to the Indians and they became again good friends.

This story gained notoriety both in England and New England, and we quote from "Hudibras," which is the name of a very satirical poem written by Samuel Butler:

"Though nice and dark the point appear,
(Quoth Ralpho,) it may hold up, and
    clear.
That *sinners* may supply the place
Of suffering *saints*, is a plain *case*.
Justice gives Sentence, many times,
On one Man for another's crimes.
Our Brethren of New England use
Choice Malefactors to excuse.
And *hang* the Guiltless in their stead,
Of whom the *churches* have less need:
As lately 't happened: In a town
There lived a *cobbler*, and but one,
That out of Doctrine could cut *use*,
And mend Men's *lives*, as well as *shoes*.
This precious Brother having slain,
In times of Peace, an Indian
(Not out of Malice, but mere Zeal,
Because he was an infidel),

The mighty *Tottipottymoy*,
Sent to our *elders* an *envoy*,
Complaining sorely of the Breach
Of League, held forth by Brother *Patch*,
Against the *Articles* in force,
Between both churches, his and ours,
For which he craved the *saints* to render
Into his Hands, or hang th' *offender:*
But they, maturely having weighed,
They had no more but him o' th' Trade,
(A man that served them in a double
Capacity, to *teach* and *cobble*,)
Resolved to spare him; yet to do
The *Indian Hoghan Moghgan*, too,
Impartial Justice, in his stead, did
Hang an old Weaver that was Bed-rid.
Then wherefore may not you be skipp'd,
And in your Room another Whipp'd?"

"WELCOME ENGLISHMEN"

A good-looking Indian, tall and erect, his face painted with red and black lines, with three eagle feathers braided into his long black hair, in his hand a long bow, and a quiver of arrows slung over his shoulders, one day in March, 1621, appeared in what is now called Leyden Street, Plymouth, and addressed the surprised and frightened Pilgrims with these well-known words, "Welcome, Englishmen." He was the first Indian to appear within the settlement. We "marvelled at it," wrote Bradford. He "caused an Alarm, he very boldly came all alone and along the houses straight to the Randevous," to quote a chapter in "Mourt's Relation," probably written by William Bradford himself, "where we intercepted him, not suffering him to goe in as vndoubtedly

1621. Welcome, Englishmen! The greeting of Samoset, the first Indian visitor to Plymouth

Photographed from a calendar issued by the New England   Kindness of Frank T. Partridge, Vice-President of
Mutual Life Insurance Company of Boston in 1890   the New England Mutual Life Insurance Company

SAMOSET, THE FIRST INDIAN VISITOR TO PLYMOUTH, MASSACHUSETTS

Greeting the Pilgrims with the surprising and now famous words, "Welcome, Englishmen!" His visit was made in March, 1621. He was a native of Pemaquid, Maine, and had learned a few English words from the fishermen who had come over from England. He later introduced Squanto and Massasoit to the Pilgrims.

he would, out of his boldnesse, hee saluted vs in English and bad vs wellcome, for he had learned some broken English amongst the English men that came to fish at Monchiggon" (now Monhegan off the coast of Maine and not far from Rockland). His name was Samoset, and he was a native of Pemaquid, Maine; probably he and his friend Squanto sailed to Cape Cod with Captain Dermer, and he doubtless lingered thereabouts until the Pilgrims arrived. "He sayd he was not of these parts," continues Mourt's chapter, "but of Morattiggon (Monhegan) and one of the Sagamores or Lords thereof, and had been 8 moneths in these parts, it lying hence a dayes sayle with a great wind, and five dayes by land."

He had picked up some language from the crews of the English vessels that sailed to our shores to fish, and he also had doubtless learned some words from his compatriot, Squanto, a native of Plymouth, who knew the language quite well, for he had lived in London for some time, as will be described later. Samoset was therefore able to tell the colonists a great deal about the country around them, the different Sagamores, the strength of the various tribes and other interesting information. He explained also that the place where they had settled down was known as Patuxet, and that an extraordinary

plague four years before had killed all the inhabitants, so that (quoting Mourt again) "there is neither man, woman, nor childe remaining, as indeed we have found none, so as there is none to hinder our possession, or to lay claime vnto it." This curious situation doubtless afforded the Pilgrims an added pretext for making their settlement here. With their numbers greatly depleted by the hardships of winter, they were living in a state of anxiety, especially after their experience with the Nauset Indians while in Provincetown, and their worries were naturally much lessened by this welcome experience. Samoset was questioned as to his Indian friends, and this imaginary conversation is taken from "The Stories of the Pilgrims."

" 'Are your friends near here?' asked Captain Standish, the military leader of the Colony. 'Many Indians in forest,' answered Samoset. 'They bring many furs to trade with white men. Indians great hunters. White man not know how to make good trap like Indian.' " "The Pilgrims," continues the story, "looked at William Bradford and smiled. He, too, was thinking of the Indian deer trap in which he had been caught, for a short time before he happened to be out hunting and was snared by the leg and suspended in the air." As the wind by this time had begun to "rise a little, we cast a horsemans coat about him, for he was starke naked, onely a leather about his wast . . . he asked some beere, but we gave him strong water, and bisket, and butter, and cheese, and pudding, and a peece of a mallerd, all which he liked well, and had bin acquainted with such amongst the English." That afternoon was spent in conversation, and when night came they "would gladly have beene rid of him," but he was unwilling to leave. The Plymouthians decided that it would be safer if their guest spent the night on shipboard, but as the tide was low that plan had to be abandoned. He was finally put up at the house of Stephen Hopkins; while there the family watched him carefully and consequently slept but little. A bed was made for him, but he preferred to spread a deerskin on the floor and slept in front of the fireplace. It is said he was not a bit angry to notice that his hosts were suspicious of him. Needless to say, the members of the Hopkins family were relieved when morning came. In fact probably few of the colony had much rest that night.

The Pilgrims gave Samoset some presents and he left Plymouth the next morning, promising to bring some of his Wampanoag friends to them in a few days. On the very next day, which was Sunday, he again appeared with five "tall proper men," according to the particularly good description given in Mourt's chapter, "every man a Deeres skin on him, and the principall of them had a wild Cats skin . . . they had most of them long hosen up to their groynes, close made; and above their groynes to their wast another leather, they were altogether like the Irish-trouses; they are of complexion like our English Gipseys." As agreed, they left their bows and arrows a quarter of a mile from the settlement. They were kindly received by the Pilgrims and, in return, amused their hosts with songs and dancing, described by the colonists as "Anticks." The Indians returned all the tools which they had stolen from them a short time before. It

From "A Popular History of the United States," by Bryant and Gay   Permission of Charles Scribner's Sons

VISIT OF SAMOSET TO THE PLYMOUTH COLONY

being Sunday, the colonists would not barter, but urged their new friends to return soon. Samoset, however, as before refused to leave, either being ill or feigning sickness, and remained until Wednesday, when he departed after having received a variety of gifts.

Samoset returned on the following day, March 22, with Squanto, with some "skinnes to trucke, and some red Herrings newly taken." They brought with them the news that their great Sagamore, Massasoit, chief of the Wampanoags, was "hard by," with his brother, Quadequina, and sixty of their men. In an hour the "King" himself appeared with his warriors on the summit of Watson's Hill on the south side of Town Brook. Evidently neither the English nor the Natives trusted each other, therefore Squanto arranged with Governor Carver for Edward Winslow to go to them and discuss the questions of peace and trading. The colonists sent to the "King a payre of Kniues, and a Copper Chayne, with a Jewell at it. To Quadequina we sent likewise a Knife and a Jewell to hang in his eare, and withall a Pot of strong water." The messenger said that King James "saluted him with words of love and Peace," and desired especially to "confirme a Peace with him, their 'next neighbor' and 'Friend and Alie.'"

After Massasoit and his warriors had refreshed themselves, the Sagamore noticed the sword and armor of one of the Englishmen and immediately wanted to buy them. After the English left Winslow as hostage, Massasoit and twenty of his followers, without their bows and arrows, marched into the English village. The colonists retained six warriors as hostages, while Captains Standish and Allerton,

From "Lives of Famous Indian Chiefs,"   *Reproduced by permission of Norman B. Wood, of the American*
by Norman B. Wood   *Indian Historical Society, and President of the American Indian*
                          Historical Publishing Company of Aurora, Illinois

MASSASOIT AND THE PILGRIMS
The first meeting of this chieftain with the colonists was in March, 1621, about three months after their landing.

with half-a-dozen musketeers, went forward to meet the Indian delegation at the Town Brook. "Salutes" were then exchanged, whereupon the visitors were conducted to one of the houses in process of building, where, following Mourt, "we placed a greene Rugge, and three or foure Cushions, then instantly came our Governour with Drumme and Trumpet after him, and some few Musketiers."

It is even said that there was a kissing of hands, followed by a request from Governor Carver for "some strong water, and drunke to him, and he drunke a great draught that made him sweate all the while over," to quote this same authority. Food was served, and then a treaty of peace was drawn up which is carefully quoted by Bradford and also in "Mourt's Relation." The original document, unfortunately, has been lost, but we are lucky to have the wording of this first Peace Treaty made on New England soil, which was faithfully kept by Massasoit for forty years, until his death in 1661, and by his people even for some years afterwards. The six articles contained in the treaty follow:

1. That neyther he nor any of his should iniure or doe hurt to any of our people.

2. And if any of his did hurt to any of ours, he should send the offender, that we might punish him.

3. That if any of our Tooles were taken away when our people were at worke, he should cause them to be restored, and if ours did any harme to any of his, wee would doe the like to them.

4. If any did vniustly warre against him, we would ayde him; if any did warre against vs, he should ayde vs.

5. He should send to his neighbour Confederates, to certifie them of this, that they might not wrong vs, but might be likewise comprised in the conditions of Peace.

6. That when their men came to vs, they should leaue their Bowes and Arrowes behind them, as wee should doe our Peeces when we came to them.

After this agreement of March 22 had been signed by the English and marks made by Massasoit and probably by some of his chiefs, the delegation of Indians was told that "King James would esteeme of him as his friend and Alie—all which the King seemed to like well, and it was applauded of his followers, all the while he sat by the Governour he trembled for feare." We also have an excellent description, probably the best, which makes him out "a very lustie man, in his best years . . . , grave of countenance, and spare of speech." Behind his neck was a bag of tobacco, which "he dranke and gave us to drinke," a customary expression used by the Indians instead of the word "smoke." Governor Carver finally conducted Massasoit back to the Town Brook, where they are said to have embraced each other, and then the chief departed. The Pilgrims still had more entertaining to do, as Quadequina, the English hostage, and another troop of his men, now approached the rude village. This brother of Massasoit apparently disliked the guns of the colonists, and indicated by signs that he would like to have them taken away, which was done. Two of his people would have liked to spend the night, but the suggestion did not appeal to the Englishmen. One thing interested Quadequina especially and that was the trumpet, and we are told that some of his men were able to sound it as well as the white men could. Samoset and Squanto remained in the town all night, while the "King" and all his men with their wives and women lay in the woods about half a mile distant. The Pilgrims were naturally still suspicious and kept watch all this while, but there was no sign of danger. On the following morning numbers of their people came

*Photographed from the marble relief on the base of the National   Kindness of the late Percival H. Lombard
Monument to the Forefathers at Plymouth, Massachusetts*

THE FIRST TREATY

Governor Carver is seated in the foreground, with Bradford next to him. Massasoit is opposite Carver and the interpreter, Squanto, is standing between them.

From "History of the Indian Wars of New England, with Eliot the Apostle," by Colonel Robert Boodey Caverly

TREATY BETWEEN THE PILGRIMS AND MASSASOIT, MADE AT PLYMOUTH,
MASSACHUSETTS, ON MARCH 22, 1621

This was the first treaty ever entered into on New England soil. Probably no actual document
was signed, though the agreement may have been entered on the Plymouth records, the early parts of
which are missing.

back to town to urge some of the English to visit their "King," and
doubtless they were eager also to procure some food. Captain
Standish and Isaac Allerton ventured alone to visit him and were
welcomed by him.

"We cannot yet conceive," according to Mourt, "but that he is
willing to have peace with us, for they have seene our people sometimes alone two or three in the woods at worke and fowling, when as
they offered them no harme as they might easily have done, and
especially because hee hath a potent Adversary and the Narowhi-
ganseis [meaning Narragansetts], that are at warre with him, against
whom hee thinks wee may be some strength to him, for our peeces are
terrible unto them; this morning, they stayed till ten or eleven of the
Clocke, and our Governour bid them send the Kings kettle, and filled
it full of pease, which pleased them well, and so they went their way."
This fear of their rivals, the Narragansett tribe, doubtless may have
influenced Massasoit in his decision to befriend the Pilgrims; never-
theless he did make this truce at a time when with the greatest of
ease he could have made away with every settler. We must also
remember that he lived strictly up to its terms, even on several
occasions when given sufficient provocation to break the agreement.
Drake well expresses it when he says, "Not that any writing or articles
of a treaty, of which he never had any adequate idea, was the cause
of his friendly behaviour, but it was the natural goodness of his heart."

Samoset and Squanto still remained at Plymouth, the latter spending part of the day fishing for eels in the river appropriately named for this fish. He caught "as many as he could well lift in one hand, which our people were glad of, they were fat and sweet, he trod them out with his feet, and so caught them with his hands without any other instrument." Not all Indians cared for eels, according to the following story told by Ellen D. Larned in her "History of Windham County." Some of the Narragansett tribe once invited some Nipmuck tributaries to visit them by the shore, where they feasted them on delicious shellfish. Later these "fresh-water Indians," which the word "Nipmuck" means, returned the compliment, but presented their Narragansett friends with eels. The latter disliked this species of fish and considered it an insult to be asked to eat them. They taunted their hosts and then blows ensued. The Narragansetts were unarmed, and the result was that only two returned alive to their wigwams. Others of the tribe marched against the Nipmucks a short time later, but were defeated.

"Squanto continued with the Pilgrims," and as Bradford wrote, "was their interpreter, and was a spetiall instrument sent of God for their good beyond their expectation. He directed them how to set their corne, where to take fish, and to procure the commodities, and was also their pilott to bring them to unknowne places for their profitt, and never left them till he dyed." The day the redskins left, the business of the Colony proceeded as usual, and John Carver was again chosen Governor.

Many tributes to Massasoit have been written. Frederick Freeman in his "Civilization and Barbarism" says: "It was certainly fortunate for the Plymouthians that Massasoit was ready in his friendship, and that he proved to be an unsophisticated, sincere, and honorable man. Though a pagan he was a man of peace, integrity, and of much excellence of character."

Alvin G. Weeks writes that, to the Pilgrims, "this friendly visit of Massasoit and his readiness to sit with them in council, to smoke with them the pipe of peace, to form with them a defensive alliance, must have seemed like a visitation of guardian angels from an unseen shore." Elsewhere the same author states, "It is to Massasoit that we pay our tribute of respect and admiration for the manly virtues, the heroic qualities, that have endeared him to every true American who has taken the pains to analyze properly the records and acquaint himself with the facts that go to make up the beginning of American history." Virginia Baker, who wrote the story of "Sowams in Pokanoket," the chief seat of Massasoit, considers that "he has always and justly been regarded as one of the most remarkable of that group of illustrious aboriginal chieftains with whom the early white settlers of New England were associated."

We close this chapter with a few lines of a poem composed by Orah F. Snow and sung at the dedication of the Massasoit statue at Plymouth:

"Massasoit, Oh! there he stands,   To greet the pilgrim to this land,
The pipe of peace within his hand,   And welcome him with open hand."

Kindness of James W. Sweany

MASSASOIT TABLET IN TOWER IN
D. W. FIELD PARK, BROCKTON,
MASSACHUSETTS

Commemorating the purchase of this territory from the Massasoit Indians on March 23,
1649. The statement of the terms of purchase
given on the tablet is rather interesting and
amusing. The accompanying illustration on
this page shows the tower.

Kindness of Fred F. Field, Jr., Brockton, Mass.

TOWER IN D. W. FIELD PARK,
BROCKTON, MASSACHUSETTS

SQUANTO GUIDES THE PILGRIMS TO BOSTON HARBOUR

On September 28, 1621, the year after the arrival of the Pilgrims
in Plymouth, they decided to explore Boston Harbour, or Massachusetts Bay, as it was then called, "to discover and view that bay, and
trade with ye natives," as Governor William Bradford wrote in his
invaluable diary, which was presented by England to the Commonwealth of Massachusetts in the year 1897. Another contemporary
account, entitled "Mourt's Relation," mentions that the object of the
expedition was "partly to see the Countrey, partly to make Peace with
them, and partly to procure their trucke, or barter." Another reason,
undoubtedly, was to learn the strength of the Massachusetts tribe
which inhabited the borders of the bay. This interesting and accurate
work of Mourt consists of a collection of journals of the daily occur-
rences in the Colony, supposed to have been written from day to
day by Robert Cushman, John Robinson, William Bradford and
Edward Winslow. G. Mourt undoubtedly stands for George Morton.
Winslow himself probably wrote the account of the voyage to
Massachusetts Bay.

Captain Myles Standish was the leader of the party, which consisted
of thirteen persons, and Squanto was chosen as their guide "to bring
us to speech with the people and interpret for us." In their shallop,

or open sail boat, were also two other Indians to act as assistants. Squanto, as everyone interested in Pilgrim history knows, was one of the three Indians who made possible the existence of this infant colony in New England.   The voyagers left Plymouth just before midnight, but as the wind was light and the distance greater than they figured, it was late in the day when they arrived at the "bottome of the Bay," as Mourt's Journal described it.   They passed Point Allerton and came to anchor off Thompson's Island.   Authorities differ as to where the "bottome of the Bay" was, but the prevailing opinion seems to fix this spot as Squantum, where they anchored and spent the night.   Early the next day their Indian guides landed Captain Standish and his followers on Squaw Rock, or Squantum Point, at Squantum, in the northern part of Quincy.   This peninsula, commanding a beautiful view of the harbour and Quincy Bay, is now owned by the City of Boston and is used as a site for a pumping station. Here has been placed a large cairn to commemorate the landing of Myles Standish and his followers, who, guided by Squanto, were the first white men to tread on Quincy soil.   The party soon found themselves in the "Massachusetts Fields" near Moswetusett Hummock, or "Sachem's Knoll," the chief seat of Chickatabot, the Sachem of the "Moswetusett," or Massachusetts Tribe.   During the Tercentenary celebration of 1930, this location was marked by a wooden sign, placed at the junction of the Squantum Road and the Quincy Shore or Wollaston Beach Boulevard.   A picture of this marker will appear in another volume.   Roger Williams, the leading authority for the origin of the derivation of the word Massachusetts, states that it is an Indian word, "et" or "ett," and may be translated as "place of." The first syllable comes from "Massi" signifying "many," while the second syllable comes from "chu" meaning "hill," giving us "the country of many hills."

The Pilgrims must have been "slenderly provided" or else "had not yet breakfasted," as Charles Francis Adams wrote in his chapter on "The Earliest Explorations and Settlement of Boston Harbour"; for "Mourt's Relation" records that "There we found many Lobsters that had beene gathered together by the Saluages, which we made ready under a cliffe."   These they made use of for their rather rich morning meal. Leaving a guard over their small vessel, Standish with Squanto and four of the English started to search for the aborigines.   They

Photographed for the State Street Trust Company

CAIRN PLACED ON SQUANTUM POINT TO COMMEMORATE THE LANDING OF MYLES STANDISH AND HIS FOLLOWERS UNDER GUIDANCE OF THE FAITHFUL INDIAN SQUANTO, ON SEPTEMBER 30, 1621

It is believed that this is the first place in Quincy ever trod by white men.   This peninsula, now the property of the City of Boston and used as a site for a pumping station, overlooks Boston Harbour and Quincy Bay. Thompson's Island is to be seen at the left.

had proceeded only a short way when they came upon the unfortunate squaw who was the owner of the devoured lobsters. They told her they had consumed her property, and, as Mourt further expresses it, "contented her for them." She gave the name of her s a c h e m as Obbatinewat, who probably lived north of the Neponset River at Savin Hill, or Dorchester Heights. Squanto set out with this Indian woman, while the rest of the company followed in the shallop. S o o n they discovered Obbatinewat and learned from him that he was under Massasoit, and that he dared not stay very long in one camp for fear the Tarratines, from Maine, would attack them at harvest time, steal their corn and kill them. He was also much in dread of Squaw-Sachem, also of the Massachusetts Tribe, and the widow of Nanepashemet. She had recently moved inland to Wachusett Mountain and married Webbacowet, a great medicine man of the nation.

SQUANTO

From a bronze statue in Pilgrim Hall, Plymouth, Massachusetts.   Kindness of A. S. Burbank

SQUANTO, FRIEND, INTERPRETER
AND GUIDE OF THE PILGRIMS
FROM MARCH, 1621, TO THE TIME
OF HIS DEATH IN DECEMBER
OF THE FOLLOWING YEAR

He acted as guide on the first visit of the Pilgrims to Sowams, Massasoit's seat in Warren, Rhode Island, and also on their voyage to Boston Harbour in the autumn of the year 1621. More of his interesting career is recorded elsewhere in this booklet. Squantum gets its name from this Indian.

Obbatinewat treated the visitors very kindly and promptly submitted to King James, as nine chieftains had done only seven days before at Plymouth. "Againe we crossed the Bay which is very l a r g e," according to Mourt's Journal, "and hath at lest fiftie Ilands in it." They admired very much the bay itself and also these islands, which were covered with trees, but which, though formerly inhabited, were then deserted. It was nightfall when the explorers reached the mouth of the Mystic River, where the Indian scouts were set ashore, but discovered no one. They decided, thereupon, to "rid at Anchor aboord the Shallop," as the same authority puts it.

Near here, at the mouth of Charles River, there was a general rendezvous of Indians, and according to Hutchinson, Lieutenant Governor of Massachusetts, "That circle, which now makes the harbours of Boston and Charlestown, round by Malden, Chelsea, Nantasket, Hingham, Weymouth, Braintree, and Dorchester, was the capital of a great sachem (referring probably to Chickatabut), much reverenced by all the plantations of Indians round about, and to him belonged Neponset (now Milton), Punkapog (now Stoughton), Wessagusett

(now Weymouth) and several places upon Charles River, where the natives were seated."

On October 1st, the next morning, all but two of the party landed and tramped inland towards Medford and Winchester, led by their Indian guides. Having gone about four miles, they came upon the place where Nanepashemet, the King of the Massachusetts Tribe, and at one time the most powerful sachem in New England, had lived from the time he left Lynn in 1615, until his death in 1619. According to the accounts left by the Pilgrims, his house was different from the usual wigwam and consisted of a large scaffold set on poles and planks about six feet above the ground, and upon this rested his hut. The location of this structure was at Rock Hill in Medford. A short distance away, near Mystic Pond, they found his stronghold, consisting of a palisaded enclosure, forty feet or so in diameter, and within they discovered a fort in which the "King" himself lay buried.

Still farther on was another dwelling, where he had been killed two years before by the warlike Tarratines. Near here the party discovered some Indian squaws, who after a short time, gained their courage sufficiently to boil some codfish and other edibles for the newcomers. Soon a male Indian was induced to show himself, "shaking and trembling for feare." The men, too, were finally appeased, and soon entered into a trade for furs. As for the Squaw-Sachem, she was too far away to be visited, so the explorers wended their way back to their shallop in the harbour. Before leaving, the Indian women who had accompanied them became so eager to barter that they "sold their coats from their backes, and tyed boughes about them, but with great shamefastnesse for indeed they are more modest," wrote Mourt, "than some of our English women are."

The Pilgrims recorded that the harbours were excellent for shipping. They were particularly impressed with the beauty and advantages of Boston Harbour, for Bradford (who may have been one of the party) entered in his diary: "They returned in saftie, and brought home a good quantity of beaver, and made reporte of ye place, wishing they had been their seated; but it seems ye Lord, who assigns to all men ye bounds of thier habitations, had apoynted it for an other use." The expedition encountered fair weather and moreover had been successful. Bradford says they "found kind entertainment" there. The colonists reached Plymouth just before noon on the following day. Charles Francis Adams declares this to have been the first recorded exploration of Boston Harbour. He considered that John Smith had only "looked into it" and Champlain wrote only a few lines concerning it.

WEETAMOE, THE QUEEN SACHEM OF POCASSET

The name "Weetamoe" came into international prominence when one of the yachts that contended for the honor of defending the *America's* Cup, in 1930, bore the name of this influential Wampanoag Indian queen. Perhaps the owners of the famous racing craft selected this name in the hopes that she might battle the English as stubbornly as did the Queen Sachem Weetamoe in King Philip's War.

The name "Weetamoe" is the Indian word for "sweetheart." This name was also bestowed on the old Howe estate in Bristol, Rhode Island. Weetamoe was the successor and probably the daughter of Corbitant, sachem of the Pocasset tribe, who had dwelt at Mettapoiset, now Swansea. Few persons have delved into the interesting history of this "Warrior Queen," or the "Squaw Sachem of Pocasset," or "Queen of the Wampanoags," to mention some of her many titles. Pocasset is the Indian name for the territory now including Tiverton and Fall River, where this able and powerful woman had her domain.

One of her camps was situated a little way from the shore on a high hill, north of the old Howland Ferry or Bridge, where now stands the stone bridge over the Sakonnet River. Her other domicile was south of Fall River, on the north side of Pocasset Cedar Swamp, between South Watuppa Pond and the heights that look down Mount Hope Bay. Near here was an Indian colony, for many years called Indian Town.

Weetamoe exercised such an influence against the colonists that Rev. Increase Mather said of her that she "was next unto Philip in respect to the mischief that hath been done, and the blood that hath been shed in this Warr." The Old Indian Chronicle containing a letter composed by a "Merchant of Boston" and communicated to a Friend in London stated that "She is as Potent a Prince as any round about her, and hath as much Corn, Land and Men at her Command. She willingly consented, and was much more forward in the Design and had greater Success than King Philip himself." Another writer on Indian subjects, Ebenezer W. Peirce, speaks in these terms: "Every inch a queen was Namumpum, alias Tatapanum, alias Weetamoe, and no untoward circumstances, no losses or discouragements, were found sufficient to quench her spirit, conquer her determination, or crush her will. . . ." Her first of many husbands was probably Wequiquinequa and they took up their abode on a neck of land now part of Tiverton, Rhode Island. They sold this property in 1651 and, as Massasoit ruled over them, it was necessary to confer with him, and, as Mr. R. F. Haffenreffer of Mount Hope, the owner of many interesting Indian relics, points out: "Perhaps this was the first time that Weetamoe saw the son of her sovereign. . . . Who shall ever know! Certainly Alexander and Weetamoe met on this momentous 21st of July, 1651—perhaps Alexander, the son and heir of the old chief sachem Massasoit, was impressed with the charm and beauty of the young Indian woman . . . perhaps Weetamoe compared the dashing young royal prince with her husband and perhaps the comparison was not satisfactory."

During 1652 she married Wamsutta, who, at the request of his father, Massasoit, had been renamed by the English, Alexander. A younger son, Metacomet, had his name changed at the same time to Philip, who was destined to be the leader of the great Narragansett war against the colonists. The Governor of Plymouth undoubtedly chose these two names as having represented the two great Macedonian heroes. When Massasoit died, Weetamoe became Queen of the Wampanoag Indians.

The first time the people of Plymouth had the opportunity to meet Weetamoe was in October, 1659, when she presented herself before

the court to enter a complaint against her husband, Wamsutta, for having sold, six years previously, some lands which she claimed belonged really to her, and for which he had never paid to her her share. This argument was amicably adjusted, but another difficulty soon arose between these two, the wife this time claiming that her husband had sold some of the lands without her consent. She again repaired to Plymouth in June, 1662, probably a few months before her husband's death, complaining of some infringement on her rights in connection with a sale of land at Saconet. The court in this case "engaged to doe what they could in convenient time for theire reliefe." Evidently things were not running very smoothly in their "wigwam" at that time.

From a print in the Indian Collection of R. F. Haffenreffer at Mount Hope, Rhode Island

WEETAMOE ENDEAVORING TO CROSS THE TAUNTON RIVER IN RHODE ISLAND

The English attacked her camp at Gardner's Neck in Swansea in August, 1676. She escaped, and while attempting to cross the river, probably on a raft, she was drowned and her body found on the Mettapoiset shore from which she had just set out.

Shortly after Wamsutta's death, his widow, without losing much time, married an Indian called Quiquequanchett, and as Mr. Haffenreffer writes, "began to entertain lavishly, inviting many Narragansett Indians to her house parties," much to the dislike of her brother-in-law, Philip, who had now become the leader of the tribe. In a few years she procured another husband called Petananuet or Petonowowet, often corrupted into Peter Nunnuit, and familiarly known to the English as merely "Ben." This new spouse she was better able to manage at home; but their politics, as one might say today, were widely different, for he sided with the English and proved of great value to them, whereas she, after much uncertainty, quite naturally threw in her lot with her brother-in-law King Philip, who had married her sister Wootonekanuske. She made this decision in spite of the fact that she had been well received at Plymouth some years before. Her husband, at the conclusion of the war, was given the responsible duty of taking charge of the prisoners of war captured by the English.

Captain Benjamin Church, who fought many successful battles against the Indians of New England, visited Weetamoe and her husband, Peter, at her Pocasset camp at Tiverton, Rhode Island, in June, just before the outbreak of hostilities. He first met the husband, who had just come over from Mount Hope in a canoe and who told him that war would surely break out in a short time. Church, at the request of this Indian, then visited the wife, who was encamped on a hill north of Howland's Ferry, which ran at one time between Tiverton and the Island of Rhode Island. She told the English that her warriors had gone to Philip's War dance, which, she said, annoyed her very much and made her melancholy. Church had recently

contrived to win over to his side Awashonks, the "Queen Sachem of Sogkonate," as she was called, and, believing he had also succeeded in obtaining the friendship of Weetamoe, hastened back to Plymouth to report his success. King Philip in the meantime persuaded Weetamoe that her former husband had been poisoned by the English, which of course was not the case, and so managed to induce her to throw her fortunes on his side during the coming conflict. We are also told that she feared her three hundred warriors would desert her unless she joined forces with her countrymen. It is indeed surprising that any Indians took sides with the colonists against their own kind, and that they proved faithful to the English under trying circumstances.

Weetamoe and her men now followed Philip in his wanderings until the fight of July 30, 1675, when the Wampanoags escaped from a swamp and retired into the Nipmuck territory for safety. Her whereabouts were uncertain until she joined the Narragansetts and Wampanoags in their fort at South Kingston, just previous to the "Swamp Fight" of December, 1675. Upon her return from the Nipmuck country she had pitched her wigwams on the west shore of the Titicut, or Taunton River in Mettapoiset, not far from Fall River. During the early days of this Narragansett War, in the autumn of 1675, she divested herself of her fourth husband and secured still another spouse, called Quinnapin or Quanopen, a Narragansett Chieftain, nephew of Miantonomo, and cousin of Canonchet, which union bound together the Narragansetts and the Wampanoags. Quinnapin was second in command at the swamp fight against the English and took part in the attack on Lancaster during the early part of 1676. He was finally captured and, after a court martial held at Newport on August 24th of the same year, he was shot on the following day.

Gradually King Philip began to lose his warriors and consequently his power, and the Queen Sachem also lost her prestige through the desertion or death of her followers, until her company consisted, it is said, of less than a sixth of her original force. She therefore decided to return to her former territory, and went to Mettapoiset in Swansea. In August of the year 1676, a friendly Indian came to Taunton and informed the English of the location of her camp, with the intention of surprising her and her warriors. Accordingly, twenty soldiers volunteered for the undertaking and succeeded in capturing thirty-six of her Indians, but she herself managed to escape. While attempting, however, to avoid the English, she was drowned as she was endeavoring to cross the river to Pocasset, and was found on the Mettapoiset shore from which she first set out.

Her death, which occurred six days before that of Philip, is best described by Rev. Increase Mather: "Now here it is to be observed that God himself by his own hand brought this enemy to destruction. For in that place, where the last year, she furnished Philip with Canoos for his men, she herself could not meet with a canoe, but venturing over the River upon a Raft, that brake under her, so that she was drowned, just before the English found her. Surely Philip's turn will be next."

This prophecy was soon to be fulfilled. The enemy cut off her head, carried it to Taunton, and set it upon a pole, according to the custom of those days. Some Indian prisoners saw it soon after, and as Cotton Mather relates, "They made a most horrid and diabolical lamentation, crying out that it was their queen's head." It is no wonder they were so shocked at the sight of the head of their devoted leader.

We have an especially interesting description of the appearance and life of this Sachem Queen through Mrs. Mary Rowlandson, who was captured in the Lancaster raid. She was sold by her captor to Quanopen and served as lady-in-waiting to Weetamoe, one of the former's three wives. Mrs. Rowlandson wrote an account of her captivity and from it we quote the following description of her mistress, one of the very few and best descriptions of a New England Indian that has come down to us:

"My master had three Squaws, living sometimes with one and sometimes with another. Onux, this old Squaw at whose wigwam I was, and with whom my master had been these three weeks. Another was Wettimore, with whom I had lived and served all this while. A severe and proud dame she was; bestowing every day in dressing herself near as much time as any of the gentry of the land: Powdering her hair and painting her face, going with her necklaces, with jewels in her ears, and bracelets upon her hands. When she had dressed herself, her work was to make girdles of wampom and beads. The third Squaw was a younger one, by whom he had two Papooses. By that time I was refreshed by the old Squaw, Wettimore's maid came to call me home, at which I fell a weeping. Then the old Squaw told me, to encourage me, that when I wanted victuals, I should come to her, and that I should lie in her wigwam. Then I went with the maid, and quickly I came back and lodged there. The Squaw laid a mat under me, and a good rug over me; the first time that I had any such kindness shewed me. I understood that Wettimore thought, that if she should let me go and serve with the old Squaw, she should be in danger to lose (not only my service) but the redemption pay also. And I was not a little glad to hear this."

A few days later upon the occasion of a dance after the attack on Sudbury, the same writer gives this further description of Weetamoe:

"She had a kersey coat, covered with girdles of wampom from the loins upward. Her arms from her elbows to her hands, were covered with bracelets, there were handfuls of necklaces about her neck and several sorts of jewels in her ears. She had fine red stockings, and white shoes, her hair powdered, and her face painted red, that was always before black. And all the dancers were after the same manner. There were two others singing and knocking on a kettle for their musick. They kept hopping up and down one after another, with a kettle of water in the midst, standing warm upon some embers, to drink of when they were dry. They held on till almost night, throwing out wampom to the standers-by."

Virginia Baker has given us this attractive sketch of Weetamoe: "Her kingdom was but a narrow strip of territory, her subjects only a handful of untutored savages. But her domain was fair and fertile; her people loyal, and never was royalty worn with a more royal grace

than by this dusky princess of the primeval forest." Again we quote Mr. Haffenreffer: "She lost her life in a desperate struggle for her race. She knew the pride of birth, the thrill of love, the sense of power. She lived strenuously and died struggling, perhaps the most interesting and the most glorious flower of Indian womanhood."

In a book entitled "Yamoyden," written by a youth twenty-two years of age, the author treats of King Philip's War, which contains some lines picturing a supposed dream of this sachem in an attempt to evade the ghostly form of his unfortunate sister-in-law, Weetamoe:

"Then thought the Sachem that his way
Through Metaposet's forest lay.
Mid the thick shadows of the grove,
A form was rushing seen;
He saw with wildered paces rove
Pocasset's warrior queen.
As from the water's depths she came,

With dripping locks and bloated frame.
Wild her discoloured arms she threw
To grasp him; and as swift he flew,
Her hollow scream he heard behind,
Come mingling with the howling wind.
'Why fly from Wetamoe? she died,
Bearing the war axe on thy side.'"

We venture to include an anecdote occasionally connected in error with Weetamoe. The King's daughter in this story was undoubtedly the offspring of Passaconaway, an Indian sorcerer who resided in the Merrimac Valley. It is narrated that her marriage to Winnepurket, Sachem of Saugus and son of Nanepashemet, took place in 1662 amidst festivities never before equalled thereabouts. A gay lot of Indians escorted the beautiful bride from her father's home at Pennacook, now Concord, New Hampshire, where "the bark-builded wigwams of Pennacook stood" (to quote the words of Whittier) to her husband's home. Some time later the youthful wife decided to pay a visit to her father, and Winnepurket sent an escort with her which is said to have been worthy of a queen. When she was ready to return to Saugus her father for some reason did not deem it essential to furnish a similar escort, but instead dispatched a messenger to her husband to repair to Pennacook and take her back himself. This his son-in-law highly resented, declaring: "When she departed from me, I caused my men to escort her to your dwelling, as became a chief. She now having an intention to return to me, I did expect the same courtesy in return." Passaconaway is reported to have become very angry and, according to Drake, the husband and wife at once separated.

AMERICAN INDIANS IN LONDON

There was so much interest and curiosity shown by the people of England in the first American Indians to appear in London and elsewhere that Shakespeare, in writing "The Tempest" about the year 1610, introduces a character called Trinculo, who makes the remark, "Were I in England now as once I was, and had but this fish painted, not a holiday fool there but would give a piece of silver: there would this monster make a man; any strange beast there makes a man: when they will not give a doit to relieve a lame beggar, they will lay out ten to see a dead Indian."

One of the oldest original documents pertaining to England and the American Indian is a letter found in the Colonial office records in the Public Record Office, London, by Richard Holworthy of London, who

ETOW OH KAOM, KING OF THE RIVER NATION OF CANADA, ONE OF THE FIVE IROQUOIS TO VISIT QUEEN ANNE IN LONDON IN 1710

The *Spectator* printed an article supposed to have been written by one of these Indian "Kings," and another London magazine records their visit to that city. They were conveyed in the Queen's coaches to St. James's to meet Her Majesty. They landed in Boston on their return to America. The name of this Chief is spelled in various ways. This is probably the same Indian as Hendrik.

assisted in compiling much of the foreign material in this chapter. This letter, dated 1607, was written in Latin by George Popham, President of the Second Colony of Virginia, addressed to his "most heigh and mightie my gratious Soveraigne Lord James of Great Britain Frannce Ierland and Virginia." He asserts in this letter that the original inhabitants declare that there is a sea not more than seven days' journey from Fort St. George in Sagadahoc (Maine) which must be the Southern Sea leading to China. Another sentence mentions that "Fahanida (Dehamda) one of the natives who has been to Britain has published here your virtues and your praises to them. To what extent I should be of value in undertaking these affairs and in strengthening the courage of the natives may be left to the judgment of those who have discussed the matter at home."

Many years later Dean Swift in his Journal to Stella, dated London, April 28, 1711, noted: "The Spectator is written by Steele with Addison's help; 'tis often very pretty. Yesterday it was made of a noble hint I gave him long ago for his Tatlers about an Indian supposed to write his travels into England." Swift later complained because all the "under hints" he gave him were published in the "Tatler" of May 13, 1710, thereby preventing his writing a book on that subject.

About a year later the "Spectator" printed an article supposed to have been written by one of the five Iroquois "Kings" called Saga Yean Qua Prab Tom, who in the spring of 1710 journeyed from Canada, under the guidance of Colonel Schuyler, First Mayor of Albany, to visit their "Great Queen" Anne, "to relate to her those Things we thought absolutely necessary for the Good of her and us her Allies." This story refers to an upholsterer with whom these "Kings" or "Princes" lodged while in London, and it was through him that this amusing and possibly unauthentic account of their impressions of England was supposedly discovered, parts of which we quote.

"On the most rising part of the town (London) there stands a huge house, (St. Paul's), big enough to contain the whole nation of which I am king. Our good brother Etow Ob Kaom, king of the rivers, is of opinion it was made by the hands of that great god to whom it is

From "*A Popular History of the United States,*" by Bryant and Gay   Permission of Charles Scribner's Sons
INDIANS IN LONDON

consecrated. The kings of Granada, and of the six nations, believe that it was created with the earth, and produced on the same day with the sun and moon.

"The queen of the country appointed two men to attend us, that had enough of our language to make themselves understood in some few particulars. But we soon perceived these two were great enemies to one another, and did not always agree in the same story. We could make a shift to gather out of one of them, that this island was very much infested with a monstrous kind of animals, in the shape of men called Whigs; and he often told us, that he hoped we should meet with none of them in our way, for that, if we did, they would be apt to knock us down for being Kings. Our other interpreter used to talk very much of a kind of animal called a Tory, that was as great a monster as the Whig, and would treat us as ill for being foreigners. These two creatures, it seems, are born with a secret antipathy to one another, and engage when they meet as naturally as the elephant and the rhinoceros.

". . . we often saw young, lusty, raw-boned fellows carried up and down the streets in little covered rooms by a couple of porters, who are hired for that service. Their dress is likewise very barbarous, for they almost strangle themselves about the neck, and bind their bodies with many ligatures, that we are apt to think are the occasion of several distempers among them, which our country is entirely free from. Instead of those beautiful feathers with which we adorn our heads, they often buy up a monstrous bush of hair, which covers their heads, and falls down in a large fleece below the middle of their backs; with

Photographed from a print in the British   Kindness of Richard Holworthy of London
Museum for the State Street Trust Company

THE IROQUOIS CHIEFS WHO VISITED QUEEN ANNE IN 1710

Showing their message to their "Great Queen." Etow Oh Kaom, undoubtedly Hendrik, is shown in several other illustrations. Portraits of these four chiefs were painted in London by I. Verelst and prints were made from them by John Bowles & Son of Cornhill, London.

which they walk up and down the streets, and are as proud of it as if it was of their own growth. We were invited to one of their public diversions, where we hoped to have seen the great men of their country running down a stag, or pitching a bar, that we might have discovered who were the persons of the greatest abilities among them; instead of that, they conveyed us into an huge room lighted up with abundance of candles, where this lazy people sat still above three hours to see several feats of ingenuity performed by others, who it seems were paid for it.

"As for the women of the country, not being able to talk with them, we could only make our remarks upon them at a distance. They let the hair of their heads grow to a great length; but as the men make a great show with heads of hair that are none of their own, the women, who they say have very fine heads of hair, tie it up in a knot, and cover it from being seen. The women look like angels, and would be more beautiful than the sun, were it not for little black spots that are apt to break out in their faces, and sometimes rise in very odd figures. I have observed that those little blemishes (beauty patches) wear off very soon; but when they disappear in one part of the face they are very apt to break out in another, insomuch that I have seen a spot upon the forehead in the afternoon, which was upon the chin in the morning."

"Charing Cross and its Immediate Neighbourhood" states that these visitors lodged in King Street, Covent Garden, at the house of the musician Dr. Arne's father, an upholsterer, who hung out the sign of the "Two Crowns and Cushions." This residence was supposed to have been next door to the Garrick Club. Fortunately for these Indians it did not burn down until a short time later. They were well received by the people of London and by royalty, for one writer states that "The carrying of four (one having died) Indian casaques about in the queen's coaches, was all the triumph of the Harleian administration; they were called kings, and clothed by the playhouse tailor like other kings of the theatre." Their success was even noted by a New York historian, who says: "The arrival of these five sachems in England made a great bruit throughout the whole kingdom. The mob followed wherever they went, and small cuts of them were sold among the people." There are also pictures of them in the British Museum, one of which we reproduce, King Etow Oh Kaom, probably the same as Hendrik. They were conveyed to St. James's, where they had an audience with the Queen.

In a speech they declared "they had with one consent hung up the kettle and taken in their hands the hatchet, in token of their friendship to the Great Queen and her children," to quote from the "Charing Cross" article. "These Kings told the Queen, plainly, that if she was not mindful of them they and their families must forsake their country, and seek other inhabitations, or stand neuter," continues the article.

Of course the usual presents of wampum belts followed. They even offered "to run down a Buck or Stag before the Queen, when she pleases to see them, in any of her Parks or Chaces. They are to tire down the Deer, and catch him without Gun, Speare, Launce, or any other Weapon"—so reads the booklet containing a description of their

visit, printed in London in 1710. Prolonging their stay, they were given a sail in one of her Majesty's ships, were entertained by the Duke of Ormond, who held a review for their benefit, and after seeing most of London, they repaired to Portsmouth, sailing from S p i t h e a d on *H.M.S. Dragon,* with a convoy of eighteen sail bound for America. They reached Boston on July 15, 1710.

Interest in things Indian was shown recently when the Royal Choral Society produced in London an opera dramatized from Longfellow's "Hiawatha," in which two American Indians took part. This "Hiawatha" celebration has been held for the past six years. These various references show clearly the interest taken by the English in our Indians, the earliest of whom were, unfortunately, kidnapped, and carried away from

Photographed from Palmer's "History of Lake Champlain." Kindness of H. M. Lydenberg, Assistant Director of the New York Public Library

PORTRAIT OF KING HENDRIK

the shores of Canada and New England to be exhibited as curiosities for the sake of gain; or else these poor redskins were taken abroad under some pretext, to serve later as guides on other expeditions in quest of new lands, or to assist in the discovery of new fishing grounds or gold mines in this country.

As long ago as the first voyage of Columbus to America, we find that this explorer took back with him to Spain a number of Indians, of whom several died on the return voyage and seven were presented to the King. One of those who died had been baptized and is said to have been the "first of his race to enter heaven." Following Columbus, Sebastian Cabot of Bristol, England, took three natives from Newfoundland in 1502 and exhibited them as curiosities at the Court of Henry VII. According to Rapin "they were clothed with the skins of beasts, and lived on raw flesh, but after two years (residence in England), were seen in the king's court clothed like Englishmen, and could not be discerned from Englishmen."

Harris wrote: "In the 14th Year of King Henry VII (1498–9) there were three Men brought to the King, . . . who were cloathed in Beast-Skins, eat raw Flesh, spoke a strange uncouth Tongue, and were very brutish in their Behaviour"; but he further adds, that he "saw these People himself two years afterwards, and that they were then cloathed like Englishmen; and he could not have known them to be otherwise, if he had not been informed that these were the men brought over by Sebastian Cabot." They were brought to court "in their country habit," according to Berkeley and were undoubtedly the first American Indians ever seen in England. In 1500 a Portuguese, called

Cortereal, kidnapped several Indians and sold them into slavery. A few years later, in 1508, the French, under Captain Thomas Aubert, discovered the St. Lawrence River, and carried several natives back to Paris, the first ever to be seen in France. It is also said that Verazzini, another French discoverer, succeeded in capturing an Indian boy, probably from some port in Connecticut. Still another well-known voyager, Jacques Cartier, by stratagem and force took captive from the St. Croix River, in 1535, a chief called Donacona, who died soon after reaching France. Captain Frobisher took a native to London in 1576.

The first American Indians taken to England, of whose names we are definitely certain, were Manida, Skettwarroes, Dehamda, already mentioned, Assacumet, and the well-known Squanto, or Tisquantum, the "Tongue of the Pilgrims," as he is often described. This last and most important Indian, a native of Plymouth, became a friend of the Pilgrims and lived with them until he died in 1622. These five natives were captured deceitfully and by force by Captain George Waymouth, who in 1605 was sent to New England on a trading expedition by Sir Ferdinando Gorges, at that time commander of the Port at Plymouth. This English navigator was in search of the Northwest Passage to India, and landed on our shores probably near Pemaquid in Maine.

James Rosier, "a gentleman employed in the voyage," wrote an account in his "True Relation of the Most Prosperous Voyage" and narrated their method of capturing these peaceful redskins, who took the newcomers by the hand, set them down by their fire, and gave them tobacco. Two of the natives were enticed on board ship by means of food; the other three were secured on shore. They were first offered presents, but as this method did not banish their fear, "We used little delay," wrote Rosier, "but suddenly laid hands upon them. And it was as much as five or six of us could doe to get them into the light horseman. For they were strong and so naked as our best hold was by their long haire on their heads." He further explains that they would not have done them harm, as they desired to make use of their knowledge of the country. Having gotten their five captives, including two canoes, and many bows and arrows, Rosier then

Photographed for the State Street Trust Company from a print in the British Museum
Kindness of Richard Holworthy of London

OLD HENDRIK, SACHEM OF THE
MOHAWK TRIBE OF INDIANS

In his court dress. He swore allegiance to the King of Great Britain, and visited London in 1710 with four other Indian chiefs or "Kings." He was killed in a battle near Lake George while fighting on the same side with Sir William Johnson, leader of the English forces in North America.

makes this entry: "Our captain had two of them at supper with us in his cabin to see their demeanor, and had them in presence at service: who behaved themselves very civilly, neither laughing nor talking all the time, and at supper fed not like men of rude education, neither would they eat or drink more than seemed to content nature; they desired pease to carry ashore to their women, which we gave them, with fish and bread, and lent them pewter dishes, which they carefully brought again."

Waymouth arrived in Plymouth, England, in July of this same year, whereupon Gorges took three of the natives, Manida, Skettwarroes, and Squanto, into his own family, the other two being installed in the household of Sir John Popham.   Rosier makes no mention of Squanto. According to Gorges, Squanto (or some Indian with a similar name) resided with him three years and was taught English. From him he learned much about New England, and began to lay plans for another expedition here.   Gorges explains that "they were all of one nation but of several parts and several families. This accident must be acknowledged the meanes, under God, of putting on foote and giving life to all our Plantations"; and later he says: "After I had those people sometimes in my Custody, I observed in them an inclination to follow the example of the better sort; and in all their carriages manifest showes of great civility fare from the rudenesse of our common people." . . . "And having kept them full three yeares, I made them able to set me downe what great Rivers ran up into the Land, what Men of note were seated on them, and what power they were of, how allyed, what enemies they had," etc. These Indians were introduced to the Court of King James.

Sir Ferdinando sent Henry Challons to America the following year in the *Richard* of Plymouth, and with him went Manida and Assacumet. This vessel was captured by a Spanish fleet, "and both my natives lost," stated Gorges. Assacumet, sometimes known as Sassacomoit, afterwards found his way back to England somehow, and eight years later voyaged to New England with Captain Hobson, in company with two other Indians, Epanow and Wanape. Chief Justice Popham despatched Captain Martin Pring from Bristol in search of Challons, and with him sailed Dehamda and Skettwarroes, the former sent by John Popham, and the latter by Gorges. These two natives proved excellent guides, and the latter returned again to England with Pring, who obtained much valuable information. On this expedition was an English boy who played the guitar to the Indians, and we learn that they enjoyed the music so much that they danced around him and heaped presents of all kinds upon him. There were two mastiffs also on board, which had quite the opposite effect, frightening the natives most horribly. The following year, 1607, they piloted the first New England colony to the mouth of the Kennebec River. This expedition under Captain Gilbert proved a failure, and not wishing to use violence, these two Indian guides were permitted to remain behind in their own country and we hear no more of them.

Squanto, the fifth Indian taken to England by Waymouth, had an interesting career, which cannot however be definitely determined owing to incomplete data. He went to England twice and possibly

three times. One excellent authority, J. P. Baxter, believes that in
1614 he was brought back to Cape Cod by Captain John Smith, as
an interpreter, and that Smith left him here, hoping some day to
return and gain through him the good will of the natives. We do
know definitely that Thomas Hunt, who came over with Smith,
captured in April, 1614, an Indian called Squanto, or Tisquantum,
among the twenty-four or so Patuxets and Nausets, whom he betrayed
and conveyed to Spain to be sold as slaves. The redskin probably
led his companions on board, as he had been accustomed to trust the
English. Some of these Indians were sold in Spain and others were
reported seized. After several years of danger and hardship, Squanto
was fortunate to get aboard an English ship in Malaga, and found
his way to Conception Bay in Newfoundland, according to Mr. Baxter.
From there he was probably taken to Cape Cod and then later to
England by Captain Thomas Dermer, who was also in this country
at that time. The Governor and Council, in their Relation printed in
1622, confirm this statement. Somehow this Indian seems to have
gotten to England, as we learn that a year later he was living with
John Slaney, or Slaine, a merchant in Cornhill, London, where he
resided for about two years. His host was one of the undertakers of
the Newfoundland plantation and Treasurer of the Company. While
in England, Squanto seems to have been kindly treated, for we read
in "The British Empire in America," printed in London, that Mr.
Slaney "used him so well, that nothing but the Love of Liberty and
his own Country could invite him to quit his Service." While in
London he was taught the English language. He returned to New
England in 1619, or possibly earlier, with Captain Dermer, who was
employed by Gorges. With this captain he traveled to Middleboro,
acting as interpreter when occasion required his services, and later he
fell in with the Pilgrims at Plymouth.

Governor Bradford makes the definite statement in his "History of
Plimouth Plantation," that Squanto made one voyage over and back;
and if by chance Gorges was correct in the statement that Waymouth
brought him over earlier, this Indian may have crossed the Atlantic
three times. Most authorities believe that Gorges made an error in
the name. Bradford wrote that he was a "native of this place, & scarce
any left alive beside him selfe. He was caried away with diverce
others by one Hunt, a m^r. of a ship, who thought to sell them for
slaves in Spaine; but he got away for New-foundland & other parts
& lastly brought hither into these parts by one Mr. Dermer, a gentleman imployed by S^r. Ferdinando Gorges & others, for discovery."

Bradford may have forgotten the possible intermediate voyage.
In any event Squanto and his compatriots had interesting experiences,
pictured rather graphically by Herbert Milton Sylvester in his "Indian
Wars of New England." "One can imagine the savage Nahanda
(Dehamda), Epanow and Squanto as they gathered about their
wigwam fires, Ingram-like, relating the stories of their wanderings, and
of the strange peoples and stranger things they had seen in their
captivities—tales as strange to them as the tales of the Thousand
and One Nights have seemed to the present-day reader. Squanto was
a good story-teller, and no doubt his auditors were lost in amaze and

felt their hearts chill with strange fear as they saw the hull of the adventurous Englishman, growing larger and ever larger, upon the horizon of the Great Waters."

To go back some years, we read that in 1611 Edward Harlow, who was another of Gorges' captains, at Monhegan Island in Maine, seized three natives, by name Pechmo, Monopet and Pekenimne. Pechmo escaped by jumping overboard, and later stole up with his companions, cut the small boat adrift, took it ashore and prevented the English from recovering it. Drake declares that this deed was "as bold & daring, . . . as that performed in the harbor of Tripoli by our countryman Decatur." From here Harlow sailed southward to an island called by the Indians Nohono, where he captured a native named Sakaweston, who was taken to England where he lived many years. He was a soldier in the wars of Bohemia, wrote Captain John Smith, and it has never been ascertained whether he ever returned.

Proceeding farther south, this English captain put in at Marthas Vineyard, and he took two more natives, Coneconam and Epanow, making five in all to be taken captive to England. Of the latter we know a good deal, for he was clever and managed to escape, as we shall see. Gorges writes about him: "How Captaine Harley (Harlow) came to be possessed of this Savage, I know not, but I understood by others how he had been showed in London for a wonder, it is true he was a goodly man of a brave aspect, stout and sober in his demeanor, and had learned so much English as to bid those that wondered at him, 'Welcome, Welcome,' this being the last and best use they could make of him, that was now growne out of the peoples wonder." Later on Gorges states: "At the time this new Savage [Epanow] came unto me, I had recovered Assacumet, [already referred to] one of the Natives I sent with Captain Chalownes [Challons] in his unhappy imployment, with whom I lodged Epanaw, who at the first hardly understood one the others speech, till after a while."

These two Indians contrived a plan to escape from England. They explained that on Epanow's island gold might be found in abundance and Gorges was induced to send another expedition in search of this rare mineral. Accordingly, Captain Hobson set sail in June, 1614, taking with him these two Indians and a third called Wanape, a native sent to Gorges from the Isle of Wight, where he doubtless had been living after having been conveyed to England from our shores. Arriving at the harbour of Marthas Vineyard, where Epanow lived, this crafty redskin, in spite of every precaution, managed to escape with the connivance of his compatriots, who came out in twenty canoes, and shot a volley of arms at the visitors. "The gold dream vanished," as one writer put it. A short time later Epanow again "got even" with the English. As we have seen, Captain Dermer came to New England in 1619, and met this native of Capoge (Indian name for Marthas Vineyard), and we will let Gorges tell in his own words of what followed.

"Dermer met with the savage who had escaped, of whom before. This savage, speaking some English, laughed at his own escape, and reported the story of it. Mr. Dormer [Dermer] told him he came

From an engraving in the collection of the State Street Trust Co.

CAPTAIN SMITH RESCUED BY POCAHONTAS

from me, and was one of my servants, and that I was much grieved
he had been so ill used as to be forced to steal away. This savage
was so cunning, that after he had questioned him about me and all
he knew belonged unto me, conceived he was come on purpose to be-
tray him, and conspired with some of his fellows to take the Captain.
Thereupon they laid hands upon him; but he being a brave, stout
gentleman, drew his sword and freed himself, but not without fourteen wounds. This disaster forced him to make all possible haste
to Virginia, to be cured of his wounds." He died soon after. Nothing further can be learned of Monopet, Pekenimne and Coneconam,
the natives mentioned as having been captured by Harlow.

We will next mention another Indian, nicknamed Jackstraw, and
whose real name may have been Wanchese, or more probably Manteo.
If so, it is possible that Captains Amidas and Barlow, who sailed
for Raleigh, brought him to the western part of England from
Virginia. Jackstraw served in the household of Sir Walter, and he
may possibly have been the servant who, seeing his master smoking,
believed him to be on fire and threw water over him to put out
the flames. It has been said that the Indian, as a tobacco sign,
was brought out in England at this time. This Indian, Jackstraw,
was probably so named from a minister of Maidstone, who, as
Drake says, "flourished in Wat Tyler's rebellion, and whose real
name was John Ball, but afterwards nicknamed Jackstraw." We
know that a faithful Indian called Manteo was christened Lord of
Dassamonpeack as a reward for his fidelity to the English. At least
one authority, Sir Gerard Herbert, mentions that Sir Walter Raleigh

From "The Historie of Travaille into Virginia, Britannia," by William Strachey, Gent.

Courtesy of Edward Lynam, Hon. Sec. Hakluyt Society, London, England

EMPEROR POWHATAN, FATHER OF POCAHONTAS, SURROUNDED BY HIS WIVES

himself had arrived in America, that he had been well received by the Indians, some of whom were now kings, and that he actually met some whom he formerly had sent to school while they were in England. This statement appears in a letter written to Carleton on February 13, 1618. An Indian "King" living near Savannah requested to be buried on a hill near that city where he met the first Englishman, supposed by some to have been Sir Walter.

With the exception of the four "Kings" from Canada, all the Indians we have mentioned were either abducted or persuaded to go abroad. The next Indian to whom we refer was Pocahontas, daughter of the Emperor Powhatan of Virginia, the most celebrated Indian Princess in America, who went to England in a very different rôle, as the bride of John Rolfe, a well-known Londoner, "a gentleman of much commendation," as one biographer styled him. She was one of the most famous of American women, especially when one considers that she lived less than twenty-three years, and that only one of these years was spent in England. Her original name was Matoaka, signifying "snowflake," changed later to Pocahontas, meaning "a rivulet between two hills."

Captain John Smith narrates in an eloquent manner his reception in 1607 by her father, who was seated before a fire upon a platform like a bedstead, wearing a robe of raccoon skins, with "all the tayles hanging by." As Smith was brought in, everyone gave a great shout. "The Queen of Appamatuck was appointed to bring him water to wash his hands, and another brought him a bunch of feathers, in stead of a Towell to dry them: having feasted him after their best barbarous manner

From "John Smith—Also Pocahontas," by John Gould Fletcher, published by Brentano's, Inc.

Permission to reproduce given by Lowell Brentano, Brentano's, Publishers, 225 Fifth Avenue, New York City

ANOTHER VERSION OF POCAHONTAS SAVING THE LIFE OF CAPTAIN JOHN SMITH

Reproduced by permission of C. O. Buckingham, Washington, D.C.   Kindness of Raymond J. Queenin

BAPTISM OF POCAHONTAS AT JAMESTOWN, VIRGINIA, IN 1613

From a painting in the rotunda of our Capitol at Washington, D.C.

they could, a long consultation was held, but the conclusion was, two great stones were brought before Powhatan: . . . dragged him (Smith) to them and thereon laid his head, and being ready with their clubs, to beate out his braines, Pocahontas the King's dearest daughter, when no intreaty could prevaile, got his head in her armes, and laid her owne upon his to save him from death: whereat the Emperour was contented he should live to make him hatchets, and her bells, beads and copper."

The English Captain was in this manner saved by the thirteen-year-old girl, who on still another occasion divulged a plot to kill him. She also saved the life of another Englishman called Henry Spilman.

Some years later Captain Samuel Argall, through the treachery of an Indian sachem, called Japazans, and his wife, and by the promise of a copper kettle, enticed Pocahontas on board ship and with his prize set sail for Jamestown. The object of this abduction was to avert war with her father, and in this Argall was successful. This truce pleased Pocahontas and helped reconcile her to her semi-imprisonment. Sir Thomas Dale was serving at this time as Governor of Virginia, and in 1613 took Pocahontas in his vessel up York River to her father's residence in hopes of bringing about a lasting peace. For some time John Rolfe had been paying his attentions to the Princess as well as teaching her Christianity, and before long their engagement was announced. Powhatan, rather to their surprise, acquiesced, and sent her uncle and two of his own sons to witness the marriage service, which took place at Jamestown early in April, 1614. This ceremony was probably attended by many of the colonists, and

A DIFFERENT PICTURE OF POCAHONTAS SAVING
THE LIFE OF CAPTAIN JOHN SMITH

the scene was undoubtedly a picturesque one. It has been imaginatively reconstructed by the Seelyes in their book "Pocahontas": "... the odd bridal procession moved up the little church with its wide-open windows and its cedar pews. The bridegroom was a young Englishman, the bride an Indian Chief's daughter, accompanied by two red-skinned warriors, her brothers, and given away by an old uncle. Perhaps more than one of the colony's ministers officiated. Before the altar with its canoe-like font Pocahontas repeated in imperfect English her marriage vows, and donned her wedding ring. It was the first union between the people who were to possess the land and the natives."

The bride was baptized Rebecca, an event which has been shown in a painting in the rotunda of our Capitol in Washington, and which is here reproduced. Thomas Dale was pleased at this "royal" alliance because the fiercest of all the Indian tribes thereabouts, the Chickahominies, at once made a treaty and became English subjects. This Englishman tried to induce Powhatan to allow him to marry another of his daughters, whereupon the "Emperor" replied: "He cannot have my daughter. If he is not satisfied, I will move three days' journey from him and never see Englishmen more."

Rolfe and his bride lived first at Jamestown, and later moved to his plantation on the James River, known as Bermuda Hundred.

A few years after their marriage, Mr. and Mrs. Rolfe, Sir Thomas Dale, with Pocahontas'

From "Lives of Famous Indian Chiefs," by Norman B. Wood

CAPTAIN SMITH MAKING TOYS FOR
POCAHONTAS

After his life had been saved by this Indian princess.

From "A Popular History of the United States," by Bryant and Gay   Permission of Charles Scribner's Sons

PRESENTATION OF POCAHONTAS AT COURT

brother-in-law, Tomocomo, otherwise Uttamatamakin, and several other Indians of both sexes, sailed for England, reaching Plymouth on the 12th of June, 1616. A news letter mentions their landing: "Sir Thomas Dale is arrived from Virginia, and brought with him some ten or twelve old and young of that country, among whom is Pocahontas, daughter of Powhatan, a king or cacique of that country. . . . All that I can hear of it is, that the country is good to live in, if it were stored with people and might in time become commodious."

The new arrivals traveled by coach to London, and created much excitement on the way, especially Pocahontas. Tomocomo, it is said, was especially interested to see so many grain fields and trees, as he had believed that the lack of these had brought the English to Virginia. Pocahontas' brother-in-law was sent by Powhatan to England to ascertain if Smith were dead. He was directed especially to learn the state of the country and to report the number of persons he found there, also to see the "God of the English" and the King and Queen. Evidently he was put out at not being promptly received by them, for he remarked: "You gave Powhatan a white Dog, which Powhatan fed as himselfe, but your King gave me nothing, and I am better than your white Dog."

To perform part of this mission Tomocomo procured a long stick, and every time he saw anyone he proceeded to cut a notch in it. "He was quickly wearie of that taske," wrote Smith, and upon his return to Virginia reported to Powhatan: "Count the stars in the sky, the

leaves on the trees, and the sand upon the seashore,—for such is the number of the people in England." Reverend Samuel Purchas, Rector of St. Martin's near Ludgate in London, had a conversation in that city with this Indian, the details of which interview he later published in his "Pilgrims." "Hee is said also to have set up with notches on a stick the numbers of men, being sent to see and signifie the truth of the multitudes reported to his Master. But his arithmetike soone failed. . . . With this Savage I have often conversed at my good friends Master Doctor Goldstone, where he was a frequent guest; and where I have seen him sing and dance his diabolicall measures." Captain Smith also renewed his acquaintance with Tomocomo. There was evidently much curiosity to see the behaviour of this Indian, as he was more uncivilized than the others. About the same time, Powhatan gave one of his native servants, Namontack, to Captain Newport, who took him to London, leaving with the "Emperor" an English boy to study the customs of the Indians. Namontack died as he was about to be baptized.

The Princess soon found the smoke of London an undesirable contrast to the forests and pure air to which she had been accustomed, and her husband therefore moved to Brentford, about seven miles outside of the city. Captain Smith happened to be in England between voyages and, hearing that she had arrived, he went to visit her. Upon seeing him she turned away and hid her face, evidently offended at not being allowed to call him father, according to a Virginian custom. She finally said to him: "You promised my father, that what was yours should be his; and that you and he would be all one. Being a stranger in our country, you called Powhatan father; and I, for the same reason, will now call you so. You were not afraid to come into my father's country, and strike fear into every body but myself; and are you here afraid to let me call you father? I tell you, then I will call you father, and you shall call me child; and so I will forever be of your kindred and country. They always told us that you were dead, and I knew not otherwise, till I came to Plimouth. But Powhatan commanded Tomocomo to seek you out, and know the truth, because your countrymen are much given to lying."

She was apparently surprised to learn that he was still alive, and it has been stated by some that had she known he were not dead she might have married him had he cared for her. He was twenty-eight at the time of their first dramatic meeting, whereas she was only 12 or 13.

Their slight disagreement must have been soon forgotten, for Smith was able to arrange for her reception by the King and Queen. The letter he wrote to the latter, with the request that she should receive her, is in existence, in which he says that Pocahontas "was become very formall and civile after our English manner . . ." that "divers persons of great ranke and qualitie had beene very kinde to her"; and before she arrived at London, he "to deserve her former courtesies, made her qualities knowne to the Queene's most excellent Majestie and her court, and writ a little booke to this effect to the Queene." She was actually introduced to King James I and the Queen by Lord and Lady De La Ware, who accompanied her to a number of masquerades, balls, plays and other entertainments.

From a contemporary engraving in the British Museum, taken   *Kindness of Richard Holworthy of London*
from a painting now lost

POCAHONTAS, BAPTIZED REBECCA, DAUGHTER OF "EMPEROR" POWHATAN OF
VIRGINIA, THE MOST CELEBRATED INDIAN PRINCESS IN AMERICA

She became the bride of a well-known Londoner, John Rolfe, who was Secretary of the Virginia
Colony. In 1616 they went to England, where she had a great success. The newly married couple
lived first in London and then in Brentford. As they were about to return to Virginia, the following
year, Pocahontas was taken ill on shipboard while at Gravesend, and was taken ashore and died.
They had a son called Thomas, who returned to Virginia and was the ancestor of many important
families in America. This portrait appeared some years ago on one of our Government stamps.
This picture is similar to the so-called Booton Hall portrait done by Simon de Parse about 1616.
Another painting from this portrait is in the State Library in Richmond, Virginia.

Kindness of Charles Stewart of the Cunard Line, Boston, Massachusetts

HEACHAM CHURCH, KING'S LYNN, NORFOLK, ENGLAND

Which contains a tablet to the memory of John Rolfe, who was born in 1562 and married Dorothy Mason. This Rolfe was father of the John Rolfe who married Pocahontas. Rolfe took his wife, Pocahontas, to Heacham Hall, the seat of the Rolfe family; and about three hundred years later Charles Stewart, a descendant of the Rolfes and the head of the Boston office of the Cunard Line, took his American bride to visit there.

From "Lives of Celebrated American Indians," by the author of "Peter Parley's Tales"

PICTURE OF POCAHONTAS AS SHE IS SUPPOSED TO HAVE APPEARED IN LONDON IN 1616

While in London many persons asked for the privilege of meeting Lady Rebecca, or Lady Pocahontas, the daughter of a king, the Indian Princess of London. Of her popularity and bearing, Captain Smith wrote, "divers Courtiers and others, my acquaintances, hath gone with me to see her . . . and they have seene many English Ladies worse favoured, proportioned, and behavioured." One of the most interesting occasions was the presentation at Court on January 6, 1617, of Ben Johnson's Christmas Masque, which was attended by Pocahontas and her brother-in-law Tomocomo. Chamberlain of this event wrote: "On Twelfth night there was a Masque, when the new made Earl (Buckingham) and the Earl of Montgomery danced with the Queen. . . . The Virginian woman, Pocahontas, and her father's councellor (Tomocomo) have been with the king and graciously used, and both she and her assistant were pleased. . . . She is upon her return, though sore against her will, if the wind would about to send her away."

Lady Rebecca also attended a reception given in her honour by the Bishop of London, which, according to Purchas, exceeded in pomp and splendor any other entertainment of the kind he had ever witnessed. The Bishop expressed himself as being very pleased at her conversion to Christianity. Of her success in London,

From "History of the Indian Tribes of North America," by Thomas L. McKenney

Kindness of Arthur L. Ayers

ANOTHER PORTRAIT OF POCAHONTAS

From an original which was painted in London during 1616 or 1617, during her short visit there, and which is now in this country. This copy was made by the artist, R. M. Sully.

STATUE OF POCAHONTAS
ON JAMESTOWN ISLAND, VIRGINIA

Placed on the property of the Association for the Preservation of Virginia Antiquities.

the Cookes in their work on Pocahontas write: "She was the New World personified in the gracious form of a little beauty of twenty-one. She suddenly became the fashion. . . . It was a curious contrast to the first years of Pocahontas, in the Virginia woods—this fine life in London, with its rich costumes and brilliant flambeaux, its gilded coaches and high revelry; but it does not seem to have affected in any degree the simplicity of her character."

It was only natural that this "recent London success" should want to remain in England, but her husband was obliged to go to Virginia to assume his duties as Secretary of the Colony. The Treasurer of the Company had the ship *George* ready for them at Gravesend; Rolfe and his wife were on board, Tomocomo with them. The other Indians remained in England to be educated.

Pocahontas, unfortunately, was taken ill with small-pox while on board ship, and died, in March, 1617, at the age of twenty-two, probably in the hostelry or cottage which stood on the corner of Stone Street in Gravesend. And so her prophecy, "I will be forever your countrywoman," came true, and sooner than she could have expected. Captain Smith, who was about to sail for New England, spoke of her end in these terms: "Shee made not more sorrow for her unexpected death, than joy to the beholders, to heare and see her make so religious and godly an end." She was buried in the chancel of the Parish Church of St. George's at Gravesend, but, owing to the burning of this building in 1727, her grave is unknown. It is

claimed that her remains were unearthed in 1907. The present St. George Church at Gravesend contains a tablet to her memory, which is shown in an illustration.

The parish register of burials at Gravesend contains this inaccurate entry. "1616, March 21, Rebecca Wroth, Wyff of Thomas Wroth, Gent. A virginia Lady borne, was buried in the Channcell." Thomas Wroth is an error, of course, for John Rolfe. The date, 1616, New Style, would be 1617.

There is on record a petition signed by Pocahontas' only son, Thomas, addressed in 1641 to the authorities of the Colony, requesting permission to journey to the "Indian country" to visit his aunt Cleopatre, and his great-uncle Opechancanough. While John Rolfe was in Virginia, his young son was left in care of Sir Lewis Steukly at Plymouth, who betrayed Raleigh and fell into such disrepute that his charge was taken to London and educated there by his uncle, Henry Rolfe. In 1648 young Rolfe returned to Virginia, and inherited much land from his grandfather Powhatan. He served as Lieutenant in command of Fort James on the Chickahominy. He became a person of great importance in the Colony and married Jane Poythvess, leaving an only daughter Jane, who married Colonel Robert Bolling. He in turn left a son named John, and from his son, also called John, are descended the Randolph, Fleming, Gay, Eldridge and Murray families.

The Rolfe family came from Heacham, Norfolk, near King's Lynn, England, whence on a clear day the Boston "Stump" can be seen across the marsh. Charles Stewart, the head of the Cunard Steamship Company in our Boston, who is descended from the Rolfe family, tells us the interesting fact that soon after his marriage to a Baltimorian he brought his wife to Heacham Hall to visit the home of his ancestors. His wife was therefore the second American bride to enter its portals, the first having been Pocahontas, about three hundred years before.

There are several pictures of Pocahontas in existence, one copied from the original and called the Booton Hall portrait. This likeness hangs in the State Library in Richmond, Virginia. Another is by Sully and is believed to be in England. Both these pictures are reproduced in this brochure.

Powhatan was much grieved to learn of the death of his favorite daughter, but expressed much interest in his grandson, whom he never lived to see, as he himself "went to the happy hunting grounds" a year after Pocahontas. An estimate of her character was made by Rand and Mann of Corn-

This
Stone Commemorates
PRINCESS POCAHONTAS OR METOAKA
DAUGHTER OF
THE MIGHTY AMERICAN INDIAN CHIEF POWHATTAN.
GENTLE AND HUMANE, SHE WAS THE FRIEND OF THE
EARLIEST STRUGGLING ENGLISH COLONISTS WHOM SHE
NOBLY RESCUED, PROTECTED, AND HELPED.

ON HER CONVERSION TO CHRISTIANITY IN 1613,
SHE RECEIVED IN BAPTISM THE NAME REBECCA,
AND SHORTLY AFTERWARDS BECAME THE WIFE OF
THOMAS ROLFE, A SETTLER IN VIRGINIA. SHE VISITED
ENGLAND WITH HER HUSBAND IN 1616, WAS GRACIOUSLY
RECEIVED BY QUEEN ANNE WIFE OF JAMES I.
IN THE TWENTY SECOND YEAR OF HER AGE
SHE DIED AT GRAVESEND, WHILE PREPARING TO
REVISIT HER NATIVE COUNTRY AND WAS BURIED
NEAR THIS SPOT ON MARCH 21ST 1617.

Photographed expressly for the State Street Trust Company
Kindness of Richard Holworthy of London

TABLET IN ST. GEORGE CHURCH, GRAVESEND, NOW PART OF LONDON, PLACED IN MEMORY OF POCAHONTAS

Photographed from a contemporary painting   *Kindness of Charles Stewart of the Cunard Line*

PAINTING OF POCAHONTAS AND HER SON THOMAS

The only known picture of both the mother and son. It is now in Sedgeford Hall, the Dower House of Heacham Hall, Norfolk County, England. Heacham Hall was the home of the Rolfe family, ancestors of Charles Stewart, who procured this photograph for the Trust Company.

hill, who said that her name "adorns the brightest page in the history of the natives of America. In whatever light we view her character, either as a maiden, a wife, or a mother, she is equally entitled to our respect and admiration. Heroic and amiable, constant and courageous, humane, generous, discreet and pious, she combined in an extraordinary manner the virtues and perfections of both savage and civilized nature. The union of so many qualities honorable to the female sex and to the human species, should never be forgotten in forming our estimate of the American race."

A number of Indian girls accompanied Pocahontas to England and proved of considerable expense, for we read under date of May 11, 1620, that "one of the maydes . . . , who sometimes dwelt a servant with a mercer in Cheapside is now verie weake of a consumption at Mr. Gough's in the Black Friers." A short time later the court directed that "two Indian maydes havinge byne a longe time verie chargeable to ye Company" should be sent to the Summer Islands. According to Captain John Smith, several were married there.

Another Indian to die in England was Mamohet, probably the only American Indian sagamore to be buried there. He was a great-grandson of the well-known sachem Uncas, who ruled the Mohegans from his chief seat, Norwich, at the head of the Thames River, in Connecticut. Mamohet was the rightful heir after the death of Cesar Uncas in 1735, but owing to his youth he was not chosen. Ben Uncas,

Photographed expressly for the State Street Trust Company   *Kindness of Richard Holworthy of London*

ST. GEORGE CHURCH, GRAVESEND, NOW PART OF LONDON

Which replaced the former Church of St. George's, burned in 1727. Pocahontas was buried here in 1617. She is supposed to have died in the hostelry or cottage which stood near-by, on the corner of Stone Street. Her grave has never been discovered. The tablet placed in this church to her memory is placed on the inside of the pillar at the right.

Photographed expressly for the State Street Trust Company

WINDOW IN ST. GEORGE CHURCH, GRAVESEND, NOW PART OF LONDON

Kindness of Richard Holworthy of London

COMPANION WINDOW IN ST. GEORGE CHURCH, GRAVESEND, PLACED THERE IN MEMORY OF POCAHONTAS

Presented in 1914 by the Society of Colonial Dames of America in Virginia, "As a token of gratitude for services rendered to that Colony by Princess Pocahontas." A picture of Pocahontas can be seen in the lower right-hand corner of each window.

an illegitimate son of "King" Uncas, desired the position, and when the Assembly of Connecticut favoured his election, Mamohet withdrew his claim. In 1726 Ben Uncas died and his son succeeded him. About ten years later, John Mason, grandson of the Indian fighter of the same name, having been deprived of his position of Overseer of the Mohegan Tribe, and feeling that he had not been fairly treated by the Colonial Government, decided to go abroad and appeal to the King of England. Mason was in favour of Mamohet's election and it was therefore decided that they, together with one of Mason's sons, Samuel, should place the whole Mohegan situation before George II. The King referred the question to the Lord Commissioners on Foreign Trade and Plantations, but Mason unfortunately died before any decision was reached. Curiously enough, Mamohet himself was taken ill and succumbed a few weeks later, sometime during the year 1735, but we have not been able to ascertain anything of his short stay in England. The Mohegans decided to elect Mamohet their "King," and accordingly during his absence held a great dance and chose him to represent them.

PRINCESS
MATOAKA REBECKA POCAHONTAS
DAUGHTER OF POWHATAN HEREDITARY OVERKING
OF THE ALGONQUIN INDIANS OF VIRGINIA
BORN 1595 BAPTISED 1613 DIED 1617
HER ROMANTIC MARRIAGE IN 1614 TO
JOHN ROLFE
BROUGHT PEACE TO THE SETTLEMENT.
TO MARK A PICTURESQUE EPISODE
IN THE HISTORY OF TWO NATIONS
THIS MEMORIAL WAS SET UP
BY FRIENDS IN
ENGLAND AND AMERICA
1933

Kindness of Charles Stewart

MEMORIAL TABLET TO POCAHONTAS RECENTLY
PLACED IN HEACHAM CHURCH, NEAR KING'S
LYNN, NORFOLK, ENGLAND, WHERE HER HUS-
BAND'S FOREFATHERS REST

This tablet is placed above the memorial to her husband's father and mother, John and Dorothy Rolfe.
Her husband was baptized in this church and her husband's father was buried in the churchyard. It is believed
she made a visit there during her short sojourn in England. Many members of the Rolfe family were present
at the dedication of this tablet, which was presented by
friends and descendants of Pocahontas in America, who
also gave a sum towards the restoration of the edifice.

On August 21, 1929, the corner stone of a memorial boulder in the Royal Burying Ground of the Mohegans, on Sachem Street in Norwich, Connecticut, was dedicated to Mamohet, who was destined never to rule, and the Lord Mayor of Norwich, England, deemed the occasion of sufficient importance to be present. One of the descendants of the tribe presented a token to the English representative, who thanked the members of the tribe for the favors shown the English so many years ago, for Uncas had been an ally of the colonists.

Another Indian to make a pilgrimage to England was John Dunn Hunter, who was captured at the age of three by a hostile tribe of I n d i a n s and brought up by them. He was given the name of Hunter on account of his prowess in the chase. Later in life he bought a farm and became interested in agriculture. He heard that Thomas William Coke, Earl of Leicester, and a r e s i d e n t of Norfolk, England, was a famous agriculturist, and in 1823 he determined to visit him to talk over this subject and get his latest ideas. His visit is described in the Memoirs of Sir James E. Smith, who mentions that "I introduced there Mr. Hunter, a native American, brought up among the Indians, and now going back with the noble design of improving them on the wisest and best principles." Coke of Norfolk, as the Earl of Leicester was called, was very pro-American during the Revolution, and at a Holkham sheep-shearing he told those present that every night during the war he drank the health of General Washington "as the greatest man on earth."

It is a very different story that attended the efforts, thirty or so years later, of Samson Occom, a full-blooded Mohegan Indian born

at Mohegan on the Thames, for it
was due largely to his efforts that
Dartmouth College, one of our
great New England educational
institutions, exists today. This
"Pious Mohegan," as he was sometimes called, was born in 1723,
about the time Ben Uncas the 2nd
was crowned sachem of the Mohegans, and later became famous
in both New England and Old
England, in which latter place he
achieved the distinction of being
the first Indian ever to preach. He

From a photograph   Kindness of Arthur L. Peale

MEMORIAL TO MAMOHET, IN THE
ROYAL BURYING GROUND OF
THE MOHEGANS, AT NORWICH,
CONNECTICUT

This Indian Sagamore was great-grandson of
Uncas, famous ruler of the Mohegans. Mamohet, with John Mason, went to London in 1735
to appeal to the King for his appointment as
Overseer of the Mohegan Tribe. Curiously
enough, both visitors died in England. Mamohet was chosen "King" during his absence. His
grave has never been discovered.

lived in his father's wigwam at
Mohegan until he became twenty
years of age, when he was placed
in the family of Reverend Eleazar
Wheelock, where he remained four
years, being his first Indian pupil.
Wheelock was a graduate of Yale
in 1733, his family having settled
in Dedham, Massachusetts, as
early as 1637. Soon after graduat-
ing he received aid from "The Company for Propagation of the Gospel
in New England and Parts Adjacent in America." This Society was
chartered in 1661 to succeed a defunct organization known as the
"President and Society for the Propagation of the Gospel in New England," which dated back to the year 1649. Wheelock was the minister
at Lebanon Crank, then part of Lebanon, Connecticut, where for a
time during our Revolution the Connecticut military headquarters
were maintained and where Duc de Lauzun and his French hussars
had their winter quarters. About the year 1740 Occom became a
Christian, taught school a few years later at New London, and was
schoolmaster and preacher to the Indians at Montauk on Long
Island from 1749 to 1761. His parentage is of interest. His father was
a Mohegan and his mother was a Groton Indian named Sarah who,
according to at least one authority, was a descendant of the celebrated
Uncas. Mary Fowler of the Montauk tribe became Occom's wife.

Wheelock received Occom at his home at Lebanon Crank in 1743,
along with several white students whom he was preparing for college.
It was in this way that the idea of educating other Indians was conceived, although his Indian school was not really started until 1754.
It was first known as the "Indian Charity School"; but later, in the
year 1770, the name was changed to "Moor's Indian Charity School,"
in honor of Colonel Joshua More, who had made a donation to the
cause some years earlier. The name of the donor is spelled in different ways, which causes some confusion. Strangely enough, this simple
school turned out to be the forerunner of Dartmouth College.

Occom became very much interested in this Charity School, and
someone, probably Reverend George Whitefield, made the suggestion
that this converted Indian, and a New Englander and Princeton

From *"Exercises and Addresses attending the Laying of the Corner Stone of the New Dartmouth Hall and the visit of the Earl of Dartmouth to the College"*
Kindness of Robert C. Strong

ELEAZAR WHEELOCK, FOUNDER AND FIRST PRESIDENT OF DARTMOUTH COLLEGE

While he was a minister at Lebanon Crank, then part of Lebanon, Connecticut, the Indian, Samson Occom, came to study under him. From this he conceived the idea of a school for Indians, the story of which is told in this brochure.

graduate called Nathaniel Whitaker, should together go to England and endeavor to raise funds for its maintenance. At this time John Smith, merchant then in London, urged that Whitaker be sent, declaring, "He must not stay to put on his wigg but come in his night cap." Occom kept a manuscript diary of their interesting experiences. Dartmouth College owns the part relating to his English visit, a page of which is here reproduced. The New London Historical Society and the State Historical Society of Hartford each possesses parts that describe other chapters in his life.

The two travelers set sail from Boston, on December 23, 1765, on the packet *Boston*, which was partly owned by John Hancock, who contributed five p o u n d s towards the passage money of twenty pounds. Fellow passengers were John Williams and Thomas Bromfield of Boston — "very agreeable company" wrote

Occom. Upon nearing the English coast, "we lay low," he writes, "and when we got within 200 leagues of Land's End, moderate easterly winds met us, and stopt us 20 days." The ship put in on February 3rd, and a landing was made at Brixham, south of Exeter. Occom and Whitaker made a day's journey on horseback and then by coach through Salisbury to London. These two made a curious pair, and are well described by Wilder Dwight Quint in his "Story of Dartmouth":

"The Indian was tall and athletic, with black hair hanging over his shoulders and being a minister he wore clerical clothes, and even in London attracted the attention of the populace. His companion

From Dartmouth Alumni Magazine
Kindness of Eric P. Kelley

MOOR HALL, NOW CHANDLER HALL, DARTMOUTH COLLEGE

Which served at one time as the Charity School for Indians. The building has been modernized.

was of fiery disposition . . . he possessed a c e r t a i n amount of business qualities, however, which were to be of assistance to him in his London mission."

The first night in London was spent at the house of Dennys de Berdt, a rich merchant who was much interested in the Indians of America; they then resided for two weeks with George Whitefield, who had been informed of their mission, and later they moved to a dwelling near the Temple. The two men owed their success to George Whitefield, who had met Wheelock in America. Occom preached in Whitefield's Tabernacle on F e b r u a r y 16th and aroused much interest. Whitefield believed there might be a possibility of interesting the second Earl of Dartmouth in this faraway proposition, as the latter was a devoted follower of Whitefield and his friend. The Earl of Dartmouth occupied the position of First Lord of Trade and Plantations and later became Secretary of State for the Colonies. A meeting between him and the two New England envoys was arranged, and of the event Occom made this

From a painting in the college presented by Governor Prescott, and copied from a mezzotint made in England in 1768, which in turn is a copy of a painting by Mason Chamberlin done for the Earl of Dartmouth, but now lost
Kindness of Harold G. Rugg, Assistant Librarian Dartmouth College, Hanover, New Hampshire

SAMSON OCCOM, KNOWN AS THE "PIOUS MOHEGAN"

A native of Mohegan on the Thames River in Connecticut, the first Indian pupil to study under Eleazar Wheelock. Occom and Nathaniel Whitaker went to London in 1765 and spent two and a half years soliciting subscriptions in England and Scotland to be used in promoting education at the Indian Charity School, the forerunner of Dartmouth College.

entry in his diary: "On Monday . . . Mr. Whitfield took Mr. Whitaker and I in his coach and introduced us to my Lord Dartmouth and appear'd like a Worthy Lord — indeed Mr. Whitfield says he is a Christian Lord and an uncommon one. . . ." Occom's description of London seems to be much exaggerated; doubtless that city did seem busy compared to his quiet little town on the banks of the Thames in Connecticut, where he spent the first years of his life, for he spoke of the great confusion in the streets. John Mason, on his Mohegan quest, was in London at the same time.

Whitaker proved helpful and continued to encourage his Indian friend, who became before long quite the rage in London. He remained unspoiled, although Whitefield wrote that he was afraid "his continuance in England" might "spoil him for the wilderness." Lord Dartmouth headed the subscription list with fifty pounds and this seemed to make his success assured. Even the King, George III, presented two hundred pounds to this Indian Charity School. Finally 2,169 names had been placed on Occom's list, some subscribers giving as small an amount as five shillings, and in addition 305 churches

From the only known existing photograph of the   *Kindness of Mrs. Edwin C. Fowler, and Ernest E. Rogers*
house, taken about 1883   *of the New London County Historical Society*

SAMSON OCCOM'S HOUSE AT MOHEGAN, NEW LONDON COUNTY, CONNECTICUT

Built by him for one hundred pounds in 1764–65, just previous to his visit to England to raise funds for Dartmouth College. The ell in the rear was his library. It was situated in the Mohegan Reservation near and west of the New London-Norwich Road. An Indian schoolhouse, no longer in use, now stands near the location, which can easily be seen on a rising slope of land between the road and the Thames. Upon his return from England in 1768 he stopped in Boston for one night, and left the next morning on horseback for his home at Mohegan. This rare photograph is owned by Mrs. Edwin C. Fowler, a descendant of Samson Occom and Tantaquidgeon, who still resides in the Mohegan Reservation not far from the location of Occom's home.

assisted the fund. The original subscription list has been lost, but the complete list of subscribers, headed by "His Gracious Majesty," may be seen in the fifth Narrative of a series of accounts of the school written by Wheelock, printed in London, and presented to Dartmouth by Mr. and Mrs. N. P. Hallowell. It will be of interest to Bostonians that one subscription came from Boston, England, from Robert Barlow. The Indian minister preached over three hundred sermons while in England.

On March 19th, Whitaker wrote a letter to Wheelock in New England: ". . . I have my Lord Dartmouth's (friendship) so our way to the throne is very short. . . . The kg (King) hath not seen Mr. Occom as yet because of this plagy stamp act." Finally the two visitors were invited to Parliament and saw the King, an event of which Occom makes this mention: "On Wednesday we were conducted to see the King's horses, carriages, and horsemen, and then went to the Parliament House and went in the Robing Room and saw the Crown first, and saw the King, had ye pleasure of seeing him put on his royal robes and crown. He is quite a comly man; his crown is richly adorned with diamonds, how grand and dazling it is to our eyes. . . . The attendance of King George is very surprizing; as he went to the House of Parliament, he and his glorious coach was attended with footmen, just before and behind and all around, and the horsemen just behind and before the footman, and the bells and all sorts of musickal instruments playing and the canon firing, and multitudes of all sorts of people thronging all around." The two visitors went to Westminster Abbey, the Tower of London, and called on the Archbishop of Canterbury and the Archbishop of York, but

the Bishop of Gloucester a year later would not ask them even to "sit down."

In the midst of Occom's success he was inoculated against smallpox and became quite ill. Many friends visited him continually during his illness, as the diary records: "On March 11, 1766 on Wednesday about a quarter after 3 P.M. I was innoculated by the Rev. Mr. Whitaker near Mr. G. Whitefield's Tabernacle in London. I was violently shocked with the working of the phisks and was full of pain all day. Was kindly visited by ladies and gentlemen constantly and had two doctors to do for me. On the 20th I began to break out,—and was attended like a child by my friends. I cou'dn't be taken care of better by my own relations. I had a very tender and carefull nurse, a young woman, and by the first day of April I was intirely well,—all my pocks were dried up and scabs dropt off."

Some months after recovering from his illness the two New Englanders made a tour of the western counties of England, returning to London in December, 1766, remaining in the city until March of the following year. They then visited central England and Scotland. Afterwards they made a trip to Ireland, where they were disappointed to learn that funds were being solicited there for Rhode Island College, now Brown University. In spite of this, the fund, even by the autumn

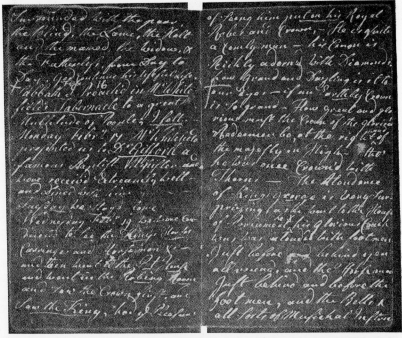

From Dartmouth Alumni Magazine   *Kindness of Eric P. Kelley*

TWO PAGES FROM SAMSON OCCOM'S DIARY

Describing his visit to the King. It also records his presence in George Whitefield's Tabernacle at the time he preached there. Most of this original diary is a valued possession of Dartmouth College, other parts being the property of the New London Historical Society, and the State Historical Society of Hartford, Connecticut.

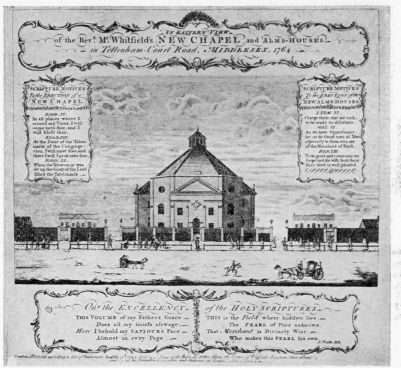

From an old print published in London in 1764   *Kindness of Richard Holworthy of London*

REV. GEORGE WHITEFIELD'S CHAPEL IN TOTTENHAM COURT ROAD, LONDON,
ENGLAND, BUILT IN 1764

Where Samson Occom preached while in England collecting funds for the Indian Charity School.
The pulpit is shown in another illustration.

of 1766, had reached the considerable sum of five thousand pounds.
When Moor's School went out of existence in 1913, there was a fund
of about $8,000 derived from other sources than English funds which
was turned over to the college treasury for the benefit of American
Indians who are qualified to carry on a Dartmouth course.

The appeal was now nearing its end, for Occom and his friend in
two years and a half had collected over 12,026 pounds, or 11,000
pounds plus expenses, a large sum for those days. The subscribers
formed a Trust and chose the Earl of Dartmouth as President. Some
complications arose among the board, but these were straightened out
and the two voyagers, pleased with their visit to the British Isles,
returned at different times, Occom embarking on the *London Packet*
and landing in Boston in May, 1768. He brought with him a number
of presents, some of which have been preserved in Connecticut. He
hastened home to Mohegan on horseback, staying in Boston only
long enough to receive hearty congratulations. He had become a
distinguished person. "Occom," wrote Mr. Quint, "had justified the
confidence imposed upon him," and well may the graduates of
Dartmouth be proud of him.

*Photographed expressly for the State Street Trust
Company. Kindness of Richard Holworthy*

PULPIT IN GEORGE WHITEFIELD'S
TABERNACLE IN TOTTENHAM
COURT ROAD, LONDON

From which Samson Occom preached during
his visit to England in 1765–68 to raise funds
to assist the Indian Charity School, later to
become Dartmouth College.

In the meanwhile, at Lebanon, Wheelock was turning out some excellent Indians and at one time had eighteen Indian scholars enrolled. The English Trust now began to look for a new and better location, and Wheelock decided upon Hanover in New Hampshire on the east bank of the Connecticut. The long and difficult pilgrimage to the new location was made during the year 1770, and consisted of a number of men on horseback, Madame Wheelock in her coach, ox-teams, negroes, one cow, and thirty students, of whom two were Indians.

When Dartmouth College was founded, the Indian school was continued as a separate institution under the name of Moor's Indian Charity School, which led a corporate existence until 1913. Dartmouth College, in theory at least, had no connection with this school, and the English Trust had no voice in the management of Dartmouth. The English trustees, although objecting to the college at first, became reconciled when it appeared that they and their funds were not to be connected with the college. The Scotch Society, responsible for funds raised in Scotland, was not so easily satisfied and retained tenaciously its funds. Grants for Indian education were made from the income for a hundred dred years and it still has the principal, which in 1920 amounted to over £10,000.

In 1904 the sixth Earl of Dartmouth, with his wife, came over to Hanover to lay the corner stone of the new Dartmouth Hall, which was to replace the building destroyed by fire that same year, and while here was given an hon-

From "A History of Montville, Connecticut," by Henry A. Baker

SKETCH OF HOUSE OF SAMSON OCCOM AT MOHEGAN,
ON THE THAMES RIVER, NEW LONDON COUNTY,
CONNECTICUT

From "*A History of Dartmouth College and the Town of Hanover, New Hampshire*," by Frederick Chase

Permission to reproduce granted by Halsey C. Edgerton, Treasurer of Dartmouth College

DARTMOUTH COLLEGE SEAL

From the pine grove, Indians are proceeding towards the building known as Moor's Indian Charity School. Between are the words "Vox Clamantis in Deserto." The figure of Religion appears on one side of the seal and Justice on the other. At the top appear the Hebrew words El Shaddae, meaning God Almighty. The motto was proposed by Wheelock to the English Trust in 1770.

From a photograph. Kindness of George H. Tripp, and William R. Herlihy, Jr., Trust Officer of the State Street Trust Company

WEATHER VANE ON THE BAKER MEMORIAL LIBRARY, DARTMOUTH COLLEGE, HANOVER, NEW HAMPSHIRE

Expressing the tradition of the College. Eleazar Wheelock, the founder and first President, is depicted as instructing an Indian under the traditional pine, under which the members of the graduating class assemble for the last time and smoke their pipes of peace after the Sachem Orator has recited his lines. The cap of the upright rod behind the figure on the left has jokingly been referred to as a keg of rum with which to instruct the Indian, carrying out the words of a famous Dartmouth song: "Eleazar was the faculty, and the whole curriculum was five hundred gallons of New England rum." Reproductions of this weather vane are also to be seen on the lamp shades of Hanover Inn.

orary degree. Lord Dartmouth revealed the interesting fact that he was a descendant of Elizabeth Washington, a great-grandaunt of George Washington. Tableaux were held and Charles A. Eastman, a Sioux and the last Indian up to that time to graduate from the College, enacted the part of Samson Occom being received by Wheelock at Lebanon in 1743, and also posed as this same Indian Minister at the time he preached his sermon in Whitefield's Tabernacle in London. Other Indians have graduated since this date of 1904. Those present also visited the grave of Eleazer Wheelock, where these words appear:

"By the gospel he subdued the ferocity   Traveller,
of the savage   Go, if you can, and deserve
And to the civilized he opened new   The sublime reward of such merit."
    paths of science—

There is a town named Occum (spelled with a "u"), just north of Norwich, Connecticut, and Occom Pond and Occom Ridge, in Hanover, delightfully commemorate this early Indian scholar, who never actually saw Hanover.

During the latter part of the seventeenth century and in the eighteenth and nineteenth centuries, there were a number of Indian delegations or missions to appear in London, and there were also numerous expeditions made by groups of Indians with the objective of making

money. In most instances a white man would plan the undertaking in hopes of helping his pocket book, promising his "American curiosities" an opportunity of seeing the sights of London, Paris, and sometimes also Belgium.

One of the most important delegations to go abroad was composed of three Cherokee Chiefs, shown in a picture, who persuaded Lieutenant Henry Timberlake, then in Virginia, to conduct an expedition to London. One of the chiefs, Ostenaco, was shown a picture of the King of England, and said, "Long have I wished to see the king my father; this is his resemblance, but I am determined to see himself; I am now near the sea, and never will depart from it till I have obtained my desires." This small party of four sailed from Hampton Roads on the fifteenth of May, 1762, arriving at Plymouth about a month later. Timberlake wrote that Ostenaco painted himself "in a frightful manner" before going ashore and as he landed "sung a solemn dirge with a loud voice, to return God thanks for his safe arrival," and that he gathered such a crowd that it was almost impossible to get to the Inn, where they took post for London. They did not seem to be as much struck with Exeter Cathedral as one would have expected, but were better pleased with Lord Pembroke's seat at Wilton, until they saw the statue of Hercules with his club uplifted, which they thought so dreadful that they begged immediately to be gone.

Upon their arrival in London they waited upon Lord Egremont, who arranged to have them lodged with N. Caccanthropos, who, much to the disgust of the visitors, charged admission to see them, thereby

From "Exercises and Addresses attending the Laying of the Corner Stone of the   *Kindness of Robert C. Strong*
New Dartmouth Hall and the visit of the Earl of Dartmouth to the College"

THE FIRST DARTMOUTH HALL, AT HANOVER, NEW HAMPSHIRE

Which was destroyed by fire in 1904. The corner stone of the new hall was laid by the sixth Earl of Dartmouth, a direct descendant of the second Earl of Dartmouth, who was the largest subscriber to the early Indian school, and first President of the Board of Trustees.

From "A History of Dartmouth College 1815–1909,"   Permission to reproduce granted by Halsey C. Edgerton,
by John King Lord   Treasurer of Dartmouth College

AN EARLY VIEW OF DARTMOUTH COLLEGE, HANOVER, NEW HAMPSHIRE

Showing the original Dartmouth Hall, which was named for the Earl of Dartmouth, who, through Samson Occom and Nathaniel Whitaker, subscribed generously to the Indian Charity School, then located at Lebanon Crank, Connecticut.

reaping, it is said, quite a harvest. As usual, the new arrivals drew large crowds wherever they went, especially at Vauxhall and Sadler's Wells Theatre. Later they were admitted to a conference with the King at St. James's. Just before the interview, Timberlake found Ostenaco preparing his pipe in order to smoke with His Majesty, according to the Indian custom. It was explained to him that he must neither offer to shake hands nor smoke with the King "as it was an honour for the greatest in the land to kiss his hand." The chief seemed surprised, but quietly acquiesced. They reimbarked on the same vessel that took them over, arriving at Charleston, South Carolina, on the 25th of August, although they had been promised that they should

From "Exercises and Addresses attending the Laying of the Corner Stone of the New Dartmouth Hall and the visit of the Earl of Dartmouth to the College" Permission of Robert C. Strong

LAYING OF THE CORNER STONE OF THE NEW DARTMOUTH HALL AT DARTMOUTH COLLEGE

By the sixth Earl of Dartmouth, who made a special journey to America to participate in this ceremony, which took place in 1904.

land in Virginia. Ostenaco declared that unless he were landed in Virginia he would not stir from London. Timberlake claimed this was not a money-making venture, but others have stated that he bought many articles which could not be used by the Indians themselves.

Towards the close of the seventeenth century the English, under Captain Allen, took as captives some Mohack (probably intended for Mohawk) Indians at York Fort in Hudson's Bay, and brought them to Plymouth, England. They were then equipped with English clothes, and furnished with wigs and swords. The complete records are to be seen in the Public Record Office in London. It seems that one Indian died at Plymouth, one was sent to Exeter, and two were retained at the former port. As only fourpence a day was allowed for their maintenance, a petition was entered for the full cost, twenty shillings. They were brought to London, and as one of them had been to France and had been well received, it was thought fitting to give more consideration to them; accordingly, as a letter from Whitehall reads, they decided to "shew those Indians all things remarkable about this Citty and more particularly His Majesty's Ship either in the River or at Chatham." After much delay they were shipped to New York, in *H.M.S. Fowey,* commanded by Captain Culliford.

The next delegation to come to our attention hailed from the South. Sir Alexander Coming in 1730 was traveling among the Cherokee nation, which was governed at that time by seven Mother Towns, and Moytoy was their Emperor. He was given this title on April 3, in the presence of Sir Alexander and twelve other Englishmen at the Chief's residence, Telliquo. So well did they think of Coming that the Emperor and his conjurers, with a concourse of warriors, "stroked him with thirteen eagles' tails, and their singers sung from morning till night." Moytoy and his leading men were required to acknowledge themselves subjects of King George, which we read, "they did on their knees, calling upon everything that was terrible to them to destroy them, and that they might become no people, if they violated their promise and obedience." On the following day a crown, five eagles' tails and four scalps were presented to Sir Alexander, with the request that he lay them at the feet of His Majesty. Moytoy asked the Englishman to choose

From "Exercises and Addresses attending the Laying of the Corner Stone of the New Dartmouth Hall and the visit of the Earl of Dartmouth to the College"
Kindness of Robert C. Strong

SECOND EARL OF DARTMOUTH, FOR
WHOM DARTMOUTH COLLEGE
WAS NAMED

THREE CHEROKEE CHIEFS WHO JOURNEYED FROM SAVANNAH, GEORGIA,
TO LONDON IN 1762

Their interpreter can be seen at the left. They were taken to England by Major Timberlake. Ostenaco, their leader, is to be seen in the centre. They interviewed the King at St. James's.

the men he desired to take with him to London, and although it was
necessary to walk four hundred miles in fifteen days to catch the man-
of-war *Fox* at Charleston, South Carolina, the delegation reached that
port in time. Skijagusta, sometimes known as Kitagusta, chief of one
of the seven Cherokee towns, as shown in an illustration, was one of
the party, the other six having such long names that we hardly have
space enough to print them.

In the short period of one month and a day the *Fox* reached Dover,
where Sir Alexander left the Indians in haste for London to arrange
for a meeting with the King, which was scheduled for June 18th. The
Indians "compared the King and Queen to the sun, the princes to the
stars, and themselves to nothing." A few days later Sir Alexander
again brought his Indian delegates before the King and his Court.
The Cherokee crown, the eagles' tails and the four gruesome Indian
scalps were offered to His Majesty, all of which it is related he was
"graciously pleased to accept of."

While in England, a treaty dated September 7th was made and
every article contained in it was accompanied by some sort of present,
such as knives or hatchets. Of course the usual speech followed, a
paragraph of which we quote: "The crown of our nation is different
from that which the great King George wears, and from that we saw
in the tower. But to us it is all one. The chain of friendship shall be
carried to our people. We look upon the great King George as the
sun, and as our father, and upon ourselves as his children. For though

we are red, and you are white, yet our hands and hearts are joined together."

Skijagusta then laid his feathers upon a table and ended with the remark: "This is our way of talking which is the same thing to us as your letters in the book are to you, and to you, beloved men, we deliver these feathers in confirmation of all we have said." Our London representative found in a London magazine an extract referring to their visit, which reads as follows: "On Wednesday the Indian Chiefs were carried from their Lodgings in King Street, Covent Garden, to the Plantation Office at Whitehall, guarded by two Files of Musqueteers. When they were brought up to the Lords Commissioners, they sang four or five Songs in their Country Language; after which the Interpreter was order'd to let them know that they were sent for there to join in Peace with King George and his People; and were desired to say if they had anything further to offer relating to the Contract they had before enter'd into. Upon which the King stood up, and gave a large Feather that he had in his Hand to the Prince, who thereupon spoke to the Lords Commissioners."

There is also an amusing account—too long to quote—in *Fog's Weekly Journal,* dated August 22 of the same year, of a visit made by some London merchants to Windsor, where they by chance ran into several members of this Indian delegation.

The well-known General James Oglethorpe, who settled Carolina, resolved to take a deputation of Georgia Indians to London in 1734, in hopes that the visit would make them firm friends of the English. Some Creeks and Yamasees had left their own tribes and settled at Yamacraw, the place where Savannah was to spring up. Tomochichi was their leader. When the English landed in Georgia numerous chiefs welcomed them, presenting Oglethorpe with buck skins, which

Photographed for the State Street Trust Company from a print in the British Museum   *Kindness of Richard Holworthy of London*

CHEROKEE CHIEFS FROM THE CAROLINAS ON A VISIT TO LONDON IN 1730

This delegation was headed by Kitagusta, the second Indian from the left. Sir Alexander Coming led the expedition, which landed in Dover, England. They met King George II, an event well described in a London magazine of that day.

*Photographed for the State Street Trust Company from
a print in the British Museum
Kindness of Richard Holworthy of London*

"KING" TOMO CHACHI, OR TOMOCHI-
CHI, LEADER OF A DELEGATION OF
YAMACRAW INDIANS FROM SAVAN-
NAH TO VISIT LONDON IN 1734

Under the guidance of General James Oglethorpe, who settled Georgia. With this Indian
chief were his wife, Senauki, his son Toonakow,
his nephew and other noted warriors. They
were introduced to the King by the Duke of
Grafton. One of the visitors died while in
London, and was buried in the cemetery of St.
John the Evangelist, Westminster. The *Gentleman's Magazine* gave a long account of their
visit. Tomochichi remained always a friend of
the English. This picture is undoubtedly from
a painting by Verelst which hung in the Geor-
gian rooms in London for many years.

one of their leaders explained were
"the best things we possess, but
we give them with a good heart."

It was arranged that fourteen
Indians, including Tomochichi, his
wife Senauki, and Toonakow, his
son, together with Hillispilli, a
noted warrior, should embark from
Charleston on the man-of-war
Aldborough. After a long voyage
of seventy days they reached the
Isle of Wight on June 16, 1734,
and hastened to equip themselves
with suitable clothes in which to
appear at court. On the appointed
day, August 1, Sir Clement Cot-
terel met them at their lodgings at
the Georgia office, with three of
the King's coaches, each drawn by
six horses, and c o n v e y e d the
visitors to Kensington, where they
were introduced to His Majesty
by the Duke of Grafton. One unfortunate redskin, whose name will
never be known, was unable to go,
for in this brief space of time he
came down with small-pox and
died the following day. Tomochichi and a few of his companions,
assisted by the upper church war-
den and one grave-digger, buried
him in the Cemetery of St. John
the Evangelist, in Westminster,
London. The burial was described
in the *Gentleman's M a g a z i n e*
under date of August 2: "One of the Indian Chiefs, Attendant to King
Tomo Chachi, died of the Small-pox. At his burial, the Corpse being
sew'd up in two Blankets, with one Deal-Board under, and another over
him, and tied down with a Cord, was placed upon the Bier, and being
laid in the Earth, his Cloaths were thrown into the Grave; after this a
Quantity of glass Beads; according to the custom of those Indians
to bury all their Effects with them." We learn that the Indians were
so sad over this bereavement that General Oglethorpe took them to his
country seat, where they remained for two weeks, bewailing their
dead companion.

At the reception in Kensington, Tomochichi appeared before His
Majesty who, according to the *Gentleman's Magazine,* was seated on
his throne. The chieftain made a speech, a few sentences of which
we copy from this magazine: "This Day I see the Majesty of your
Face, the Greatness of your House, and the Number of your People;
. . . I am come over in my old Days, tho' I cannot live to see any

Advantage to myself; I am come for the Good of the Children of all the Nations of the Upper and of the Lower Creeks, that they may be instructed in the Knowledge of the English. These are the Feathers of the Eagle, which is the swiftest of birds, and which flieth round our Nations. These Feathers are a Sign of Peace in our Land, and have been carried from Town to Town there; and we have brought them over to leave with you, O Great King, as a Sign of everlasting Peace."

Later on Tomochichi made a speech to the Queen, and the replies to both speeches have been preserved. Of their appearance, the *Gentleman's Magazine* says: "The War Captain, and other Attendants of Tomo Chichi, were very importunate to appear at Court in the Manner they go in their own Country, which is only with a proper Covering round their Waste, the rest of their Body being naked, but were disuaded from it by Mr. Oglethorpe. But their Faces were variously painted after their Country manner, some half black, others triangular, and others with bearded Arrows instead of Whiskers. Tomo Chachi, and Senauki his Wife, were dress'd in Scarlet, trimm'd with Gold."

Their visit in London is summed up in this same paper under date of October 30th: "The Indian King, Queen, and Prince &c. set out from the Georgia office in the King's Coaches for Gravesend to embark, on their return home. During their stay in England, which has been about four Months, his Majesty allow'd them £20 a Week for their subsistence, and they have been entertain'd in the most agreeable manner possible. Whatever is curious and worthy Observation in and about the Cities of London and Westminster has been carefully shewn them, and nothing has been wanting among all Degrees of Men to contribute to their Diversion and Amusement; and to give them a just Idea of English Politeness, and our Respect for them. In return they express'd themselves heartily attached to the British Nation. They had about the value of £400 in Presents; . . . They appeared particularly delighted with seeing his Highness perform his Exercise of riding the manag'd Horse, the Horse Guards pass in review, and the agreeable Appearance of Barges, &c. on the Thames on Lord Mayors day." Tomochichi was much impressed with the solidity of the London houses and seemed very surprised that short-lived people should erect such long-lived dwellings.

Tomochichi returned to his home near Savannah in the transport *Prince of Wales*, arriving late in December, 1734. He was always a friend of the English and a staunch supporter of the Colony of Georgia and often reminded his compatriots of the kindness shown them by the King. He wished to be buried among the English in Savannah, and so General Oglethorpe arranged to have him interred with military honors in a prominent location in that city. A monument to his memory has been placed in Wright Square, at or near his burial place.

A lone individual to find his way to London was King Tom Ninigret of the Niantic Tribe, who was born in 1736. He was sent to England to be educated, and an authority claims that while in London he erected a two-story house, American style. When he returned to Charlestown, Rhode Island, he put up another building

MONUMENT ERECTED TO THE MEMORY OF TOMOCHICHI, CHIEF OF THE YAMACRAWS, IN WRIGHT SQUARE, SAVANNAH, GEORGIA

This Indian Chief was companion of General James Oglethorpe and friend and ally of the Colony of Georgia. With his wife and nephew and other Indians he visited London in the year 1734. He died in 1739, at the age of ninety-seven.

known as the "Sachem's House," which stood until 1921, when it was d e s t r o y e d by fire. Mr. Chapin, of the Rhode Island Historical Society, tells us that in 1769 Ninigret visited Newport and dined with the Governor of that State. He became suddenly ill while driving near the Old Stone Mill and died at home soon afterwards.

In 1765 the *Gentleman's Magazine* records that three unnamed Cherokee chiefs were presented to the Lords of Trade and Plantations; and in the following year the magazine mentions the arrival in London of a number of Indian chiefs and their wives, representing two of the five tribes of Iroquois, with letters from Sir William Johnson. While attending church at Gravesend, ready to embark for home, a woman who had been ill struck one of the chiefs three or four blows and then scratched his wife's face, exclaiming: "You scalped my husband; you scalped my husband!" The congregation became alarmed. Some thought the church was falling, while others believed it to be on fire. All ran out, we are told, except the minister, who sat calmly until the people returned.

Another Indian visitor in London who was all-important to the English cause in America was Thayendaneca, a famous Mohawk chief, better known as Joseph Brant, which his Indian name signified. He was born in 1742 on the banks of the Ohio at Canajoharie, one of the three strongholds of the Mohawks. His father's name was Te-ho-wagh-wen-gara-gh-kwin. The son obtained his education at Moor's Indian Charity School at Lebanon, already mentioned. He received a colonel's commission in the English army. Towards the end of 1775 he decided to visit England to determine whether he should take up arms on the English side. He sailed for London with Captain Tice, who was of English extraction, though born in America. Of this first visit we know little, except that he was particularly well received and appeared at Court. He was given rooms at "The Swan with Two Necks," and was later urged to move to more suitable lodgings, but he said he preferred to remain there during his sojourn in London for the reason that the people at the Inn had treated him so kindly. James Boswell became very intimate with Brant and stated that he was a grandson of one of the five chiefs who visited London in 1710, an event already described. Boswell persuaded him to have his portrait painted, and the Earl of Warwick induced him to sit also for Romney, one of the most famous artists of that day. This latter painting is reproduced in this brochure.

After a few months' sojourn in London he returned with his friend Captain Tice, landing in New York, whence he proceeded by a hazardous journey to Canada. The Mohawk chief returned with the determination to become a firm ally of the English forevermore.

Brant's second visit to England was made in 1785, and it is said that his mission was one of great importance. On the way to London he stopped at Salisbury, where he dined with Colonel de Peister. While in the former city he met Lord Dorchester, Lord Percy, the Bishop of London and many other notables. He sat for his picture to please Lord Percy. Charles Fox presented him with a silver snuff-box, which was handed down to his daughter, who married William J. Kerr of Niagara. We are not informed as to whether the chief during his two short stays formed the European habit of taking snuff. We are told, however, that he became a great favourite with the

From "History of the Indian Tribes of North America," by Thomas L. McKenney and James Hall
Painted by Romney

THAYENDANEGEA, OR THAYENDAN-ECA, FAMOUS MOHAWK CHIEF AND CAPTAIN OF THE SIX NATIONS

Known also as Brant. He visited London in 1775 and again in 1785. He was born on the banks of the Ohio. He received an education at Moor's Indian Charity School, at Lebanon Crank, Connecticut, which was destined to be the forerunner of Dartmouth College.

royal family. When presented to the King it is said that for some reason he proudly refused to kiss his hand, remarking at the same time that he would gladly kiss the hand of the Queen. He also became intimate with the Prince of Wales, later to become George IV.

An amusing incident took place during his visit in London. A fancy dress ball was given which was largely attended. Brant was dressed in his picturesque Mohawk costume, with half of his face painted. His biographer, W. L. Stone, describes the event that followed: "He (one of the guests dressed as a Turk) scrutinized the chief very closely, and mistaking his rouge et noir complexion for a painted visor, the Turk took the liberty of attempting to handle his nose . . . the Chieftain made the hall resound with the appalling war-whoop, and at the same instant the tomahawk leaped from his girdle, and flashed around the astounded Mussulman's head. Such a piercing and frightful cry had never before rung through that salon of fashion."

King George conveyed to Brant, his ally, a tract of land bordering on Lake Ontario, where he lived in the English fashion, which did not at all please his wife, who, after her husband's death, preferred to return to the wigwam. Brant's son visited England in 1822. Rochefoucauld gives an interesting description of his visit to the residence of the chief, where he was living upon the Grand River, not far from Newark, Oxford County, Ontario: "Colonel Brant is an Indian who took part with the English, and having been in England,

was commissioned by the king, and politely treated by everyone. His manners are half-European. He is accompanied by two negro servants, and is in appearance like an Englishman. He has a garden and farm under cultivation; dresses almost entirely like an European, and has great influence over the Indians." His tomb is outside the old Mohawk Church, in Grand River, near Brantford, Ontario, formerly called Brant's Ford, a town named for this Chieftain, the greatest Indian of the Six Nations. There is also in Victoria Park of the same town a National monument erected to him by the Brant Memorial Association.

In one of the rooms of the Bath and West of England Society of Bath, England, hung for a long time a painting, by Williams, of a Mohawk Chief whose real name was Teyoninhokarawen, a name so difficult for his white friends to pronounce that they gave him the more simple title of Captain John Norton. This picture has been traced through the efforts of Richard Holworthy, and was finally discovered in the possession of Robert W. Barclay of Bury Hill, Dorking, Surrey, England, who is a great-great-grandchild of Robert Barclay of Southwark, who had it painted originally and presented to the Society in the year 1805. Captain F. G. Storr, Secretary of the present organization, at the suggestion of the State Street Trust Company, started a search and discovered this interesting vote in the records as of December 11, 1804: "The follow.g Gentlemen were elected to be Honorary Members. viz. [then follow two names] and Teyoninhokarawen, under the designation of Captain Norton, a Chief of the Mohawk Nation, who having been introduced to the Sittings of the Anniversary by R. Barclay Esq—rose and made a most appropriate Address on the occasion; in reply to which the Chairman was pleased to return to him the politest Expressions of personal Thanks." The painting was presented at a subsequent meeting held on February 12th of the following year.

While visiting Bath one day in 1804 or 1805 in his Indian costume, Norton was accosted by an Englishman who had been in America. The latter plied the stranger with questions and finally implied that he was an impostor. The Indian replied modestly and patiently, but was not able to convince the Englishman. The latter asked him how he would relish returning to the "savages of his own country." Norton quietly replied, "I shall not experience so great a change in my society as you imagine, for I find there are savages in this country also." During his busy years he translated the Gospel of St. John into his native tongue and also published an "Address to the Six Nations," which was printed by Williams & Fardon of Lombard Street, and which was now in the possession of Mr. Barclay. A London magazine states that Norton was educated at one of the American universities. Curiously enough, his mother was a resident of Edinburgh and he, himself, during his youth had spent two years there.

The last three delegations we mention were conducted through England, France or Belgium by George Catlin, a well-known expert on Indian matters, who was exhibiting a rare Indian collection in London, Manchester, and other cities in England. While in Manchester in 1845 Catlin's doorkeeper rushed in one evening announcing that there was a "homnibus at the door quite full of orrible looking folks." Nine

Ojibbeways from Lake Huron had arrived, "a pretty black-looking set of fellows" followed the former remark. Catlin was persuaded to superintend their visit in Europe and pleased them very much when he first met them with the usual exclamation of "How, how."

The first hotel to which the delegation was driven refused to take them in. The landlord asked, "What the devil is all this? . . . they're wild men, and they look more like the devil than anything else . . . load them up as quick as you please." Another inn took them in. The townspeople flocked there and caused so much damage that the proprietor declared that "It seemed to him as if the savages were all outside and the gentlemen inside." Their visit did, however, make his hostelry popular, at least temporarily. So eager were the people to catch a glimpse of even an eye or a nose of an Indian that the police soon had to be summoned. After recovering f r o m their fatiguing voyage across the "great salt lake," as they termed the Atlantic, the I n d i a n s were later taken to see Catlin's collec-

From a photograph of a contemporary painting now in the possession of Robert W. Barclay of Dorking, Surrey, England

Kindness of Richard Holworthy of London

MOHAWK CHIEF TEYONINHOKARA- WEN, KNOWN USUALLY AS CAPTAIN JOHN NORTON, WHO VISITED LONDON AND BATH, ENGLAND, IN 1804–05

This painting was presented to the Bath and West of England Society of Bath, England, by Robert Barclay of Southwark, a great-great- grandfather of the present owner. It hung in the rooms of the Society for many years. Mrs. Robert W. Barclay has sent the Trust Company a copy of a letter written by this chief in 1809, but lack of space prevents its reproduction.

tion, which was then on exhibition, and were delighted to recognize the portraits of many of their compatriots hanging on the walls. They caused much excitement in the city, as they walked about bedecked as they were wont to be in their forests. They even carried their war- clubs, bows and arrows, tomahawks and scalping-knives, and when any occurrence attracted their attention they occasionally let out a war-whoop.

Soon they visited the Mayor, or "great chief" as they called him. Shortly after their arrival one of the party noticed a great deal of smoke issuing from the mills, and ran back to his friends, remarking that the prairies were on fire. During their visits the Ojibbeways gave exhibitions of ball playing, the scalp dance, war dance, snake dance, pipe dance, and made great successes wherever they went. They were so pleased with their first effort at entertainment that the streets of Manchester resounded with their shouts and war-whoops as they wended their way back to the hotel. One day a crowd of people collected in the street and Catlin went out to ascertain the cause. Some of the Indians had discovered an exit to the roof; and the Manchester- ites believed that they had gotten loose and that it would be a hard

From "Adventures of the Ojibbeway and Ioway Indians in England, France and Belgium," by George Catlin

GROUP OF NINE OJIBBEWAY, SOMETIMES CALLED CHIPPEWAY, INDIANS FROM
LAKE HURON, CANADA

Which, in 1845, crossed the "Great Salt Lake," as the chief expressed it, to visit Manchester and London, where they were introduced to Queen Victoria. The smoke of the former city reminded them of the prairie fires at home, and they spoke of the Thames Tunnel as the "Great Medicine Cave."

matter to catch them again. Their fears were soon allayed. Some of the onlookers made their way to the adjoining roofs and some even had collected ropes and poles in order to help catch them before they could do any harm.

The delegation visited London next, being taken there by the "Iron-horse," as they termed the engine, and when it stopped to take on water they jumped out of their compartments "to see the Iron-horse drink." Upon reaching London the fog and smoke were so dense

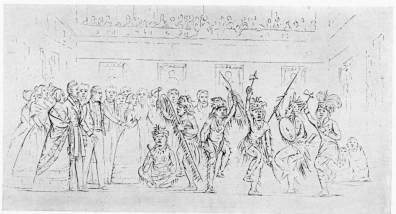

From "Adventures of the Ojibbeway and Ioway Indians in England, France and Belgium," by George Catlin

OJIBBEWAY INDIANS FROM LAKE HURON, CANADA, PERFORMING A WAR DANCE
BEFORE QUEEN VICTORIA AT WINDSOR CASTLE

Careful preparations were made for this great occasion. They were served with champagne, which the visitors called "Chick-a-bob-boo."

that they declared "the prairies must be on fire again." Of course their first duty was to hold a "Medicine Feast" and to invoke the Spirit to send them an invitation from the Queen to visit Windsor Castle, which Catlin had in his pocket several hours before the feast began. The preparations for this great occasion are well described in Catlin's book: "Colours, and ribbons, and beads, of the richest hues, were called for, and procured from various parts of the city; and both night and day, all, men and women, were constantly engaged in adding brilliancy and richness of colour to their costumes. The old chief was painting the stem of his pipe of peace (or calumet) sky-blue, emblematical of the feelings they carried in their breasts; . . . The little girl, Nibnab-e-qua, was crying, as she embroidered with red and white porcupine-quills, fearing that her new moccasins would not look so brilliant as she had sometimes made them. Her mother was arranging black mourning plumes in the cradle in which her infant had died, and which, by the custom of the country, she was obliged yet to carry on her back. The War-chief was repainting his shield, and arranging his scalps on a little hoop, to give proper effect to the scalp-dance. The Medicine-man was preparing his wa-be-no drum. Gish-ee-goshee-gee was stringing beads with his wife; and Sah-mah was brightening his tomahawk and his scalping knife for a glittering effect in the war-dance. Cadotte, during this time, was parading before the mirror, examining, arranging, and re-arranging the ostrich-plumes in his cap. . . ." An illustration shows the war dance given before Queen Victoria, who had recently become Queen. The chief, Ahqueewezaints, had carefully prepared a calumet or pipe of peace to present on this occasion, not realizing he was to appear before a Queen and not a King. He naturally became embarrassed, and not daring to give it to Prince Albert, as he was not highest in power, sadly took it back with him.

A dinner was given them at which was served champagne, called by the Indians "Chick-a-bob-boo" as it made a bubbling noise when poured out that sounded like this word. Queen Victoria sent a present of money and a piece of plaid, whereupon the chief responded: "I can't speak—I never speak. (Great applause, and he smoked again.) My friends—My heart and my tongue were never made to live together. (Roar of applause, and 'how, how, how!') Our chief is old, and his words few: he has told you that the Great Spirit has been kind to us, and that we have seen the face of our Great Mother the Queen. . . . I have no more to say, but I shall be glad in a little time to offer you my hand." Before leaving, several of the English inquired of Catlin as to how the Indians had been captured, whether with a lasso or in a pit. The party dispersed amid many remarks concerning the delicious "Chick-a-bob-boo." When the Thames Tunnel was visited they called it the "Great Medicine Cave" and proceeded immediately to give an example of the Medicine dance, which astonished the busy Londoners. An interesting event in their stay was the opening of Parliament when, from the roof of St. Mary's chapel, near Westminster Abbey, they obtained a view of the Queen in her carriage of state drawn by eight cream-coloured horses. They were sure that she looked up on the roof and had noticed them, and of course they were much gratified.

Photographed for the State Street Trust Company from a print in the British Museum

Kindness of Richard Holworthy of London

RECEIPTED BILL

of a London haberdasher for articles purchased by a delegation of nine American Indians to visit that city in 1766. Their many bills for lodging at the "Goat" in Kensington, and for their upkeep, are still preserved.

It was not very long before fourteen Ioway Indians from the base of the Rockies arrived in London and were housed at No. 7 St. James S t r e e t. Catlin welcomed t h e m after t h e i r long journey and found that he knew several, including White Cloud, the chief of the tribe. The landlady protested against their going to bed with their paint on, but it was explained to her that it was removed every night and that the Indians slept beside the beds instead of in them, which seemed to amuse and reassure the old lady very much. Some of the Londoners thought the earlier delegation had returned, while others believed they were r e a l cannibals from New Zealand.

One of the party, nicknamed Doctor, made quite a sensation as he drove on the box of the omnibus, his face painted vermilion, with a huge pair of buffalo horns above his head. The wife of Little Wolf had with her a papoose called Corsair. At one of their first exhibitions, one of their number during his address referred to London as a large

From "Adventures of the Ojibbeway and Ioway Indians in England, France and Belgium," by George Catlin

FOURTEEN IOWAY INDIANS FROM THE ROCKIES WHO, IN 1845 AND 1846, VISITED LONDON, YORK, NEWCASTLE-ON-TYNE, EDINBURGH, DUNDEE, GLASGOW, DUBLIN AND PARIS

While in London they lodged at No. 7 St. James Street. It will be noticed that of this number four were women and two were small children, one of whom died in Edinburgh and was buried at Newcastle. One of the women died in Paris. They received an invitation from Disraeli and gave an exhibition at Lord's.

From "Adventures of the Ojibbeway and Ioway Indians in England, France and Belgium," by George Catlin

IOWAY DELEGATION BEING PRESENTED TO KING LOUIS PHILIPPE, THE QUEEN, AND OTHER ROYAL PERSONAGES IN PARIS DURING THEIR VISIT ABROAD

Alexandre Vattemare, who gave to Boston the idea for the Boston Public Library, acted as their guide. One of the Indian women died in Paris and was buried in the cemetery of Montmartre.

village with many fine "wigwams," which brought forth many a good laugh from the audience. Among their first invitations was one from Disraeli, Prime Minister, and much preparation was made for the occasion. The "Doctor" spent over an hour on his toilet, and in the end was still dissatisfied with his appearance. After an examination before the looking glass he decided, according to Catlin, "that it would not do, and some bear's grease and a piece of deer-skin soon removed it all. He spent another half hour with his different tints, and, displeased again, they were all demolished as before. Alarm about time now vexed him, and caused him to plaster with a more rapid and consequently with a more 'masterly touch.' The effect was fine!" Another invitation came only a day before the dinner to which they were asked,

From "Adventures of the Ojibbeway and Ioway Indians in England, France and Belgium," by George Catlin

GROUP OF IOWAY INDIANS FROM THE ROCKIES PRESENTING AN EAGLE DANCE IN LONDON

Before their Royal Highnesses the Duke and Duchess of Cambridge, Princess Mary, and other notables.

From "History of the Indian Tribes of North America," by Thomas L. McKenney and James Hall

MOHONGO

An Osage woman, one of seven Indians from Missouri who were taken in 1827 to Holland, Germany and France by a Frenchman called Delaunay posing as an American Army officer. They were told that they would be welcome in Europe, and they were received by Charles X. They believed while going to New York that they were on the way to Washington to visit the President. These wandering natives found Lafayette, who assisted them in getting back to their native land. On the return voyage they were attacked by smallpox and three died, including the husband of Mohongo.

and they complained that it did not allow them sufficient time in which to prepare themselves for a gorge by starving beforehand and by taking tonics to increase their appetites. At church a few days later, the Doctor so far forgot himself as to light his pipe and then fall asleep. As they drove along the Serpentine one afternoon they exclaimed it reminded them of Skunk River at home. One day was reserved for an exhibition at Lord's Cricket Ground of Indian sports, including dances, archery and ball playing, wigwams b e i n g set up to make the scene more realistic. On the way to York by train the visitors were much excited to see a fox hunt and believed it was a war party in pursuit of the enemy. We will let Catlin tell in his own words the rest of the story:

"I told them they rode without guns, and the first one in at the death pulled off the tail of the fox and rode into town with it under his hatband. Their laughter was excessive at the idea of 'such gentlemen hunting in open fields, and with a whip instead of a gun; and that great chiefs, as I had pronounced them, should be risking their lives, and the limbs of their fine horses, for a poor fox, the flesh of which, even if it were good to eat, was not wanted by such rich people, who had meat enough at home; and the skin of which could not be worth so much trouble, especially when, as everybody knows, it is good for nothing when the tail is pulled off.' "

The delegation visited Edinburgh, and while there a little Indian child died and was buried at Newcastle by the Society of Friends. Dublin was visited, and then Paris, where Alexandre Vattemare, who gave to Boston the idea for our Public Library, did much for them. While there they were received by the King and the Queen, but found much difficulty in properly pronouncing "Vive le Roi!" Unfortunately, one of the Indian women, Little Wolf, died in Paris, and is said to be buried in the cemetery of Montmartre. While Catlin was still in the French Capital, another troupe of eleven Ojibbeways appeared, having come over from London. One of the most interesting incidents connected with American Indians abroad took place at St. Cloud, before the King and Queen of two royal families, the French and the Belgian. King Louis Philippe had been in America and had visited several

From "Adventures of the Ojibbeway and Ioway Indians in England, France and Belgium," by George Catlin

SECOND DELEGATION OF OJIBBEWAY INDIANS BEING PRESENTED AT ST. CLOUD,
FRANCE, IN THE YEAR 1846, TO TWO ROYAL FAMILIES, THE KING AND QUEEN
OF FRANCE, AND THE KING AND QUEEN OF THE BELGIANS

A papoose was born in the Salle Valentino, soon after the Indians arrived from London. King Louis Philippe had been to America and had visited several tribes of Indians while there. The Indians later visited Brussels and Antwerp.

tribes while here. The Duchesse d'Orléans had purchased a canoe made in this country and when this delegation arrived at St. Cloud it was apparent that their hosts were desirous of seeing a race between Indians paddling this canoe and some of their subjects in a Whitehall boat belonging to the Prince de Joinville. Below is an illustration showing this unique event, in which the Indians were outclassed,

From "Adventures of the Ojibbeway and Ioway Indians in England, France and Belgium," by George Catlin

RACE AT ST. CLOUD, NEAR PARIS, BETWEEN FOUR IOWAY INDIANS IN A CANOE
AND FOUR FRENCH OARSMEN IN A WHITEHALL ROW BOAT

In which the latter proved victorious. The canoe had been purchased in America by the Duchesse d'Orléans and the rowboat was the property of Prince de Joinville. This race furnished much excitement to the onlookers.

as their canoe was too heavily weighted with four men instead of the usual two. Three of these Indians died abroad of small-pox, which caused the death also of many others who went abroad. We will now leave the remaining Indians to find their way home to the Rockies, to meditate upon their recent experiences abroad.

An Oneida Indian called Peter Otsaquette was sent to Paris to school, where he proved an excellent pupil and became very fond of that metropolis. When he returned to his native forests in America he wore the dress of the European, which so displeased his friends that they disrobed him of his foreign apparel, compelled him to resume his Indian blanket, to grease his limbs with bear fat as was customary, and to smear his body with paint. He was forced to marry a squaw. He soon sank into intemperance, and, it is said, exchanged a portrait of Lafayette, presented to him by this illustrious Frenchman, for a bottle of rum.

Doubtless there have been other delegations of Indians in London that have not come to the attention of the writer.

THE DEATH OF CANONCHET

Canonchet, later known by the name of Nanuntenoo, son of Miantonomo, was the last great leader of the Narragansetts, and in a deed dated 1674 he was styled "chief surviving Sachem" of that tribe. This position he occupied at the time of the Great Swamp Fight, which took place during the following year and from which he was one of the very few redskins to escape. His importance at that time was expressed by Reverend Increase Mather, who wrote that he "was a principal ring leader in the Narragansett War, and had as great an interest and influence as can be said of any among the Indians," and at the time of his capture he remarked that "it was an amazing stroke to the enemy." He was feared almost as much as was King Philip himself, and his great bravery at the time of his capture cannot fail to arouse the admiration and respect of all those who appreciate rare qualities in any race of men.

During March of the year 1676, the colonists learned that Canonchet, with a force of about three hundred warriors, was setting out to attack Plymouth and the adjacent towns, whereupon Captain Michael Pierce, of Scituate, the "man who never knew fear" was sent out with seventy men to attack him. Pierce's disastrous defeat in the ensuing conflict on the west bank of the Blackstone River, in the present town of Central Falls, north of the present Pawtucket, will be mentioned in another volume. It caused the United Colonists to redouble their efforts to vanquish the enemy. The very next day four companies of volunteers from Connecticut started for the enemy's country, their most conspicuous officer being Captain George Denison of Southerton, now Stonington. To them were attached three companies of Indians, one composed of Mohegans and led by Oneko, the son of Uncas; another composed of Pequots, led by Cassasinnamon; and the other made up of Niantics, under a son of Ninigret called Catapazet. They marched through the Narragansett Country and arrived early in April at the Pawtucket, now called the Blackstone River, and not far from the

village of Pawtucket.   Here two old squaws disclosed the whereabouts of Canonchet, who was then engaged on a daring expedition to procure relief for his followers.

On a hill near-by the chief was encamped with only seven warriors. This was a rare opportunity for the English and their allies.   Canonchet had stationed two sentinels on a commanding situation, and they carried the news of the approach of the enemy, but for some reason dashed past their sachem's wigwam.   A third sentinel was dispatched to learn the cause of the flight of the other two men.   He also took to his heels, whereupon Canonchet sent out two more, one of whom reported that the whole English army was approaching, whereupon Canonchet, having no means to defend himself, fled with all the speed he possessed.   He endeavored to elude his pursuers by running around to the other side of the hill, but was recognized by the enemy, who followed him at close quarters.   In the lead was Catapazet and some of his Niantics and a few of "the English lightest of foot," as described by the author, Hubbard.   Swift as the Indian ran, his antagonists proved the swifter, and as he noticed they were gaining on him he first threw away his blanket, then his silver-laced coat, and finally his belt of wampumpeag.   The pursuers were now doubly sure that the object of their chase was Canonchet.   One of the Pequots, called Monopoide, outran his friends and came upon the chief near the river, obliging him to enter it somewhat sooner than he expected.   The result was that Canonchet's foot slipped upon a stone, causing him to stumble so as to wet his gun and render it useless.   After his capture he frankly confessed that this accident "made his heart and bowels turn within him, so that he became like a rotten stick, and void of strength."   Monopoide was enabled to seize his enemy "within thirty rods of the river side" and he became a prisoner of war.   Curiously enough, he made no attempt to escape.   One of the first to approach was Robert Stanton, a youthful Englishman, who began to question the captive.   "He appeared at first to regard the young man with silent indignity," wrote Drake, "but, at length, casting a disdainful look upon his youthful face, this manly sachem said, in broken English, 'You much child!   No understand matters of war!   Let your brother or chief come, him will I answer.'"   His capture has been so graphically described by Albert C. Greene, of Providence, in a poem, that we quote a number of his verses, in many of which the author has included the words supposed to have been uttered by the fallen chief.

"His foes are gathering fast behind,
   He feels his failing strength;
But onward strains until he gains
   A river's bank at length,
Where the deep Seekonk's winter
      stream,
   Like a cloud of feathery snow,
From the wave-worn edge of its river
      cliffs,
   Rolls down to its bed below.

"The eager host rush wildly on,—
   Where is the warrior—where?
Beside the swollen river's brink,
   Why stands he silent there?
With firm-set foot and folded arms
   He views his coming foes;
But, heedless, sees the gathering crowd
   That fast around him close.

" 'Now yield thee, Narraganset!' cried
The youngest of the band;
The captive slowly turned his head,
And proudly waved his hand.
'You are a child;—for war
You are too young and weak;
Go, let your chief or father come,
And I to him will speak!

" 'All whom he loved are dead and gone,
His people's hour is nigh;
Let all the white men load their guns;
Canonchet wants to die!'
'Thy prayer is vain; the punishment
Our righteous laws decree
To rebels and to murderers,
Must be the doom for thee.' "

Canonchet was offered his life on condition that he consider the submission of his subjects, and, wrote Hubbard, he "was as good as his word; acting herein, as if by a Pythagorean metempsychosis, some old Roman ghost had possessed the body of this western Pagan; and like Attilius Regulus, he would not accept of his own life, when it was tendered him":

" 'But send back now thy messengers,
And let there forth be brought
The Wampanoag fugitives
Who thy protection sought.
They were thy nation's enemies,
Let them thy ransom be;
Deliver them into our hands,
And thou again art free.'

'No! not one Wampanoag,—no!
My promise shall not fail!
Not one! no, nor the paring of
A Wampanoag nail!'
He threw a bitter glance of scorn
Upon the throng around,
And stilled was every motion there,
And hushed was every sound."

The English then told him he would be put to death unless he complied with their wishes, whereupon he replied that killing him would not end the war. They questioned him about his boastful speeches; his answer being that "others were as forward for the war as myself, and I desire to hear no more about it." He declared that he was born a prince, and unless a prince came to interrogate him he considered it due his honor to remain silent. The poetry continues:

" ' 'Tis good,—the Sachem then will die!
He understands it all;
His spirit hears it and is glad,
He's ready when you call.
He's glad because he'll die before
His heart grows soft and weak;
Before he speaks a single word
He were ashamed to speak.

" 'The sachem does not want to talk;
His answer you have heard;
No white man from Canonchet's lips
Shall hear another word.'
Around his tall and manly form
He wrapped his mantle then,
And, with a proud and silent step,
Went with those armèd men."

Although Canonchet requested that Oneko, who was of equal rank, should put him to death, this suggestion was not acted upon; for he was taken to Stonington, where he was shot by the Pequots, his head cut off by the Mohegans, and his body burned by the Niantics, as rewards for the faithfulness of these allies. His head was sent to Hartford, as a present for the Council. His death is recorded in the next two verses:

"The third day, when the sun had set,
The deed of guilt was o'er,
And a cry of woe was borne along
The Narraganset shore.
Through the Narraganset land a cry
Of wailing and of pain
Told that its Chief, by English hands,
Was captured and was slain.

"He bore the trial and the doom,
Scorn, insults, and the chain,
But no man, to his dying hour,
E'er heard him speak again."

The power of the Narragansetts was broken forever, although the war continued for a time under Canonicus and Quanopen.

There now remains one quotation referring to Canonchet which we would like to include, from the pen of Francis Baylies, in his "Memoir of the Plymouth Colony." He said "his whole conduct after his capture was such, that surely at this period we may be allowed to lament the unhappy fate of this noble Indian, without incurring any imputation for want of patriotism." There is a small town near Hope Valley, in Rhode Island, northeast of Westerly, near the Connecticut line, called Canonchet.

THE CAPTIVITY OF MARY ROWLANDSON

It has been thought advisable to include this story of the harrowing experiences of Mrs. Mary Rowlandson, of Lancaster, Massachusetts, chiefly for the reason that her own report of her wanderings and captivity contains interesting and valuable descriptions of Indian life and of several well-known New England Indians, including King Philip himself.

Lancaster, then known as Nashaway, was settled as early as 1643, and a tribe bearing this latter name lived near-by. Eleven years later Reverend Joseph Rowlandson, who was probably born in England about 1631, and who was the only Harvard graduate of the class of 1652, moved into the newly established settlement to assume the duties of clergyman at a salary of "fifty pounds a year, one half in wheat, six pence in the bushel under the usual price," as the record reads. His father, Thomas, died there in 1654. The Rowlandsons continued to reside in this New England town for over twenty years, and four children were born to them during that time. The youngest one, called Sarah, was destined to survive only a short time, for there was an uprising of neighboring tribes, including the Wampanoags, led by King Philip himself, together with some of the Narragansetts, his allies, joined also by a few of the Nipmucks and Nashaways. This formidable force attacked the town on February 21, 1676 (new style), and the details of this gruesome slaughter are too well known to bear repetition. At length they reached the Rowlandson homestead, which stood on an elevation on property once owned by Reverend Dr. Thayer and now belonging to Mrs. Nathaniel Thayer. The location of this house, or garrison, on the lawn of this estate is marked by a tree known to this day as the Rowlandson Pine. The Thayer property is situated near the main road that runs between Fitchburg and Worcester. Some of the attackers got behind the hill, others went into the barn or protected themselves behind some near-by shelters, and from these positions began to fire bullets into the dwelling, wounding three of the forty-two villagers who had collected there. Rowlandson himself happened to be in Boston to solicit more soldiers for the protection of the town. At the end of two hours the Indians seized upon the idea of firing the building. The flames were put out, but again they set it on fire. It was now a question of the Rowlandsons leaving their shelter or of being burned alive.

From "King Philip's War," by George W. Ellis and John E. Morris
Permission of The Grafton Press, New York City

ROWLANDSON PINE ON THE ESTATE OF MRS. NATHANIEL THAYER, IN LANCASTER, MASSACHUSETTS

Where stood the Garrison House which was attacked by Indians in the year 1676. Here Mrs. Rowlandson was captured.

"Then I took my children . . . to go forth and leave the house," wrote Mrs. Rowlandson in her "Narrative of the Captivity and Removes," "but as soon as we came to the door, and appear'd, the Indians shot so thick that the bullets rattled against the house as if one had taken a handful of stones and threw them, so that we were forced to give back. We had six stout dogs belonging to our garrison, but none of them would stir, though at another time if an Indian had come to the door, they were ready to fly upon him and tear him down."

The fire roared behind them, and they were finally compelled to come out in the open, where eighteen of the defenders were immediately killed. It has been learned that seventeen of the Rowlandson family were either killed or taken prisoners during this raid. For some reason, Mrs. Rowlandson and her youngest child, although both wounded, were told that no further harm would befall them if they would come along with them. This unfortunate woman wrote that she had often said to herself that if any Indians came upon them she would rather be killed than taken alive, "but," she continues, "when it came to the trial, my mind changed; their glittering weapons so daunted my spirit, that I chose rather to go along with those ravenous bears, than that moment to end my days." In the end she was finally rewarded. "Now away we must go with these barbarous creatures, with our bodies wounded and bleeding, and our hearts no less than our bodies," continues the narrative. The first "remove," as each chapter is entitled, was to George Hill, within sight of the town, and so called from an Indian who once had his wigwam upon it. This hill now is part of the property of John E. Thayer, Jr. There happened to be a vacant house near-by, and Mrs. Rowlandson asked permission to lodge in it for the night, to which she received the reply, "What, will you love Englishmen still?" She and her only child passed a doleful night amid the roaring, singing and dancing of the exultant Indians.

She has vividly described the motley collection of horses, cattle, lambs, pigs and fowl plundered from the people of Lancaster, some of which were being roasted or boiled to serve as a victory feast for the enemy. To add to her sorrow the Indians then told her they would surely kill her husband on his way back from the "Bay." On the following morning they turned their backs on the town and set out into the wilderness. One of the Indians held the child on a horse, while the mother trudged along on foot, and later she carried her daughter herself as long as her strength held out. Then they both were put on horseback, and, as she expressed it, "there being no 'furniture' upon

the horse's back," much to the delight of their captors they were pitched over his neck as they were proceeding down a steep hill, probably near Fitchburg. To add to the difficulties of this poor woman and her friends, it began to snow, and night found her sitting in the snow, her child having fallen into a violent fever. A new method of traveling was now found by seating the mother and child on horseback behind one of the Indians. All this time, from Wednesday to Saturday evening, neither had tasted a morsel of food. Their trail now probably led to an Indian town called Wenimesset, now New Braintree, lying north of Brookfield, thence to Miller's River.

It does not seem possible that any person could survive the hardships endured by this brave woman. Of course her baby soon died, whereupon the mother was detailed to care for Quinnapin, an important sagamore, who married the sister of King Philip's wife, called Weetamoe, concerning whom we have a separate chapter. A Narragansett Indian captured her, so she explains, and sold her to her present master. The captive by good chance met her daughter Mary, who was held prisoner at one of their stopping places, and she was also fortunate enough to have a similar opportunity of talking to her son Joseph. She then graphically describes the return of a marauding party that had burned and sacked Medfield. One of the returning Indians brought back a Bible, and, taking pity on her, presented it with his compliments.

The Indians then proceeded to Miller's River, which was crossed; thence they moved in a northwesterly direction until they reached the Connecticut River at Northfield, then known as Squaukeag. They then traveled along this river four or five miles, which probably brought them into New Hampshire. All this time Mrs. Rowlandson ate scarcely anything, merely "filthy trash," as she entered it in her diary: "On the Saturday they boiled an old horse's leg and so we drank of the broth"—which by this time she considered to be rather a delicacy. At another meeting place an Indian happened to walk by her with a basket of horse-liver. She asked him for a piece, to which he replied, "What, can you eat horse-liver?" "I told him I would try," she replied, "if he would give me a piece, which he did; and I laid it on the coals to roast, but before it was half ready they got half of it away from me; so that I was forced to take the rest and eat it as it was, . . . and yet a savory bit it was to me. . . ."

We now come to the most interesting part of the narrative, portions of which we quote: "We travelled on till night, and in the morning we must go over the river to Philip's crew. When I was in the canoe, I could not but be amazed at the numerous crew of Pagans that were on the bank on the other side. When I came ashore, they gathered all about me, I sitting alone in the midst." They were probably now in Vermont. "Then I went to see King Philip; he bade me come in, and sit down; and asked me whether I would smoke it? (a usual compliment nowadays, among the saints and sinners) but this no ways suited me. For though I had formerly used tobacco, yet I had left it ever since I was first taken. It seems to be a bait the devil lays to make men lose their precious time. I remember with shame, how formerly,

when I had taken two or three pipes, I was presently ready for another. . . . Now the Indians gathered their forces to go against Northampton: Over night one went about yelling and hooting to give notice of the design. . . . Philip spake to me to make a shirt for his boy, which I did, for which he gave me a shilling. I offered the money to my mistress, but she bid me keep it, and with it I bought a piece of horse-flesh. Afterward he asked me to make a cap for his boy, for which he invited me to dinner; I went, and he gave me a pancake, about as big as two fingers; it was made of parched wheat, beaten and fried in bear's grease, but I thought I never tasted pleasanter meat in my life.

"There was a Squaw who spake to me to make a shirt for her Sannup; for which she gave me a piece of beef. Another asked me to knit a pair of stockings, for which she gave me a quart of peas and beef together, and invited my master and mistress to dinner; but the proud gossip, because I served them both in one dish, would eat nothing, except one bit that he gave her upon the point of his knife. . . . At this place . . . what with the beams and heat of the sun, and smoke of the wigwams, I thought I should have been blinded. I could scarce discern one wigwam from another. There was one Mary Thurston, of Medfield, who seeing how it was with me, lent me a hat to wear; but as soon as I was gone, the Squaw that owned that Mary Thurston, came running after me, and got it away again. . . . The Indians returning from North-Hampton brought with them some horses, and sheep, and other things which they had taken. . . . But instead of either going to Albany or homeward, we must go five miles up the river, and then go over it"

From "Historical markers, erected by Massachusetts Bay Colony Tercentenary Commission"
Kindness of Hon. Frederic W. Cook, Secretary of the Commonwealth of Massachusetts

MARKER IN LANCASTER

To commemorate the location of Rowlandson Rock on George Hill near-by, where Mrs. Rowlandson, and the other captives taken during the Lancaster raid, passed their first night of captivity.

—back into New Hampshire. "When we were at this place, my master's maid came home: she had been gone three weeks into the Narraganset country to fetch corn, where they had stored up some in the ground. She brought home about a peck and a half of corn. This was about the time that their great captain (Naonanto) was killed in the Narraganset country." This must have been such a willing maid that walked such a distance for such a small amount of food. "I was fain to go look after something to satisfy my hunger; and going among the wigwams, I went into one, and there found a Squaw who shewed herself very kind to me, and gave me a piece of bear. I put it into my pocket, and came home; but could not find an opportunity to broil it for fear they should get it

from me. . . . I have sometimes seen bear baked handsomely amongst the English, and some liked it, but the thoughts that it was bear, made me tremble. But now that was savory to me that one would think was enough to turn the stomach of a brute creature. . . ."

"The Eleventh Remove": "The next day in the morning, they took their travel intending a day's journey up the river; I took my load at my back, and quickly we came to wade over [the cold river]. And passed over tiresome and wearisome hills. . . . It was upon a Sabbath-day morning that they prepared for their travel. This morning I asked my master whether he would sell me to my husband? he answered 'nux'; which did much rejoice my spirit. My mistress, before we went, was gone to the burial of a Papoos, and returning, she found me sitting and reading in my Bible. She snatched it hastily out of my hand and threw it out of doors: I ran out and catcht it up; and put it in my pocket, and never let her see it afterwards. Then they packed up their things to be gone, and gave me my load; I complained it was too heavy, whereupon she gave me a slap on the face and bid me be gone. . . . going out to see what I could find, and walking among the trees, I found six acorns, and two chestnuts, which were some refreshment to me. Towards night I gathered me some sticks for my own comfort, that I might not lie a cold; but when we came to lie down, they bid me go out, and lie somewhere else, for they had company. . . . I told them if I went to another wigwam they would be angry and send me home again. Then one of the company drew his sword and told me he would run me through if I did not go presently. . . . Mine eyes hath seen that fellow afterwards walking up and down in Boston, under the appearance of a friendly Indian, and several others of the like cut. . . . We were at this place and time about two miles from Connecticut River. . . . I told them the skin was off my back, but I had no other comforting answer from them than this, that it would be no matter if my head was off too. . . . Instead of going towards the Bay (which was what I desired) I must go with them five or six miles down the river. . . . I had not seen my son a pretty while, and here was an Indian of whom I made enquiry after him, and asked him when he saw him? He answered me, that such a time his master roasted him, and that himself did eat a piece of him as big as his two fingers, and that he was very good meat. . . .

"And here I cannot but remember how many times, sitting in their wigwams, and musing on things past, I should suddenly leap up and run out, as if I had been at home, forgetting where I was, and what my condition was; but when I was without, and saw nothing but wilderness and woods. . . . About this time, I began to think that all my hopes of restoration would come to nothing. I thought of the English army, and hoped for their coming, and being retaken by them, but that failed. I hoped to be carried to Albany, as the Indians had discoursed, but that failed also."

They were probably now in the vicinity of Charlestown near the Connecticut. "I thought of being sold to my husband, as my master spake; but instead of that, my master himself was gone, and I left behind, so that my spirit was now quite ready to sink. . . . About this time they came yelping from Hadley, having there killed three English-

men, and brought one captive with them, viz. Thomas Read. They all gathered about the poor man, asking him many questions. I desired also to go and see him; and when I came he was crying bitterly, supposing they would quickly kill him. Whereupon I asked one of them, whether they intended to kill him, he answered me, they would not: He being a little cheered with that, I asked him about the welfare of my husband; he told me he saw him such a time in the Bay, and he was well, but very melancholy. By which I certainly understood (though I suspected it before) that whatsoever the Indians told me respecting him, was vanity and lies. Some of them told me he was dead, and they had killed him: some said he was married again, and that the governor wished him to marry, and told him that he should have his choice, and that all persuaded him I was dead." The meeting with Read was therefore rather a curious coincidence.

"Hearing that my son was come to this place, I went to see him, and told him his father was well, but very melancholy: . . . Then my son came to see me. . . . So his master carried him away, and I never saw him afterward, till I saw him at Piscataqua in Portsmouth. . . . Now must we pack up and be gone from this thicket, bending our course toward the bay-towns. . . . We came to Baquaug (or Miller's) River again that day, . . . We began this remove with wading over Baquaug River (near Orange or Athol). The water was up to our knees and the stream very swift, and so cold, that I thought it would have cut me in sunder. . . . I got up to go along with them. Quickly there came up to us an Indian who informed them that I must go to Wachuset to my master, for there was a letter come from the council to the Saggamores about redeeming the captives, and that there would be another in 14 days, and that I must be there ready. My heart was so heavy before, that I could scarce speak, or go in the path; and yet now so light that I could run. My strength seemed to come again, and to recruit my feeble knees and aching heart; yet it pleased them to go but one mile that night, and there we stayed two days. In that time came a company of Indians to us, near thirty, all on horseback. My heart skipt within me, thinking they had been Englishmen, at the first sight of them: For they were dressed in English apparel, with hats, white neckcloths, and sashes about their waists, and ribbons upon their shoulders: . . . At night we came to an Indian town, and the Indians sat down by a wigwam discoursing, but I was almost spent and would scarce speak. I laid down my load, and went into the wigwam, and there sat an Indian boiling of horse-feet (they being wont to eat the flesh first, and when the feet were old and dried, and they had nothing else, they would cut off the feet and use them). I asked him to give me a little of his broth, or water they were boiling in; He took a dish, and gave me one spoonful of samp, and bid me take as much of the broth as I would. . . .

"Then we came to another Indian town, where we stayed all night. In this town there were four English children captives, and one of them my own sister's. I went to see how she did, and she was well, considering her captive condition. . . . Then I went into another wigwam, where there were two of the English children: The Squaw was boiling horses' feet, she cut me off a little piece, and gave one of the

English children a piece also. Being very hungry, I had quickly eat up mine; but the child could not bite it, it was so tough and sinewy, but lay sucking, gnawing, and slabbering of it in the mouth and hand, then I took it of the child, and eat it myself, and savory it was to my taste. . . . They said when we went out, that we must travel to Wachuset this day. (This town is Princeton, Massachusetts, near Wachuset Mountain.) But a bitter weary day I had of it, travelling now three days together, without resting any day between. At last, after many weary steps, I saw Wachuset hills, but many miles off. . . . Going along, having indeed my life, but little spirit, Philip (who was in the company) came up, and took me by the hand, and said, Two weeks more and you shall be mistress again. I asked him if he spoke true? he said yes, and quickly you shall come to your master again, who had been gone from us three weeks. After many weary steps, we came to Wachuset, where he was, and glad was I to see him. He asked me when I washed me? I told him not this month; then he fetched me some water himself, and bid me wash, and gave me a glass to see how I look'd, and bid his Squaw give me something to eat. So she gave me a mess of beans and meat, and a little ground-nut cake. I was wonderfully revived with this favour showed me." The Indian Chief also offered her a pipe which she declined, as she had "overcome her former appetite for tobacco," as the Farmers' Almanack expressed it.

In Princeton, not far from the base of Wachuset Mountain, is a huge ledge, which has been named "Redemption Rock" to commemorate the release of Mary Rowlandson, for on that spot on May 2, 1676, John Hoar of Concord, Massachusetts, and this band of Indians made an agreement which secured her freedom. A tablet was placed here by Honorable George F. Hoar.

Reverend Mr. Rowlandson and several other ministers all this while were using their best efforts to bring about her freedom through the Council. This body ordered Major Daniel Gookin—who with John Eliot had helped many of the Christianized Indians—to procure from the Indian internment camp on Deer Island several of the prisoners to approach the Indians at Princeton. None would, however, undertake this difficult mission, though Gookin did his best to persuade them. Towards the end of March the Council was again petitioned and another attempt was made. Gookin told Rowlandson that a certain Tom Nepanet was inclined to accept and Captain Daniel Henchman, who was supervisor over some of these interned Indians, was ordered to treat with him, finally getting him to leave the Island a few days later. This Indian then repaired to the house of Daniel Gookin in order to be fitted out for the enterprise.

He departed with the first note which was written by Governor Leverett of Massachusetts at the request of the Council, asking for a release of all the men, women and children then in captivity, desiring an answer in writing, and enclosing "paper, pen and incke" for that purpose. Before Mrs. Rowlandson obtained her release, several interesting letters were exchanged, parts of which are worth including. This was the reply brought back by Tom Nepanet:

"Answer brought back April 12.

"We nou give answer by this one man, but if you like my answer sent one more man besides this one Tom Nepanet, and send with all true heart and with all your mind by two men; because you know and we know your heart great sorrowful with crying for your lost many many hundred man and all your house and all your land and woman child and cattle as all your thing that you have lost and on your backside stand. Signed by Sam, Sachem; Kutquen and Quanohit, Sagamores; Peter Jethro, scribe. Mr. Rowlandson, your wife and all your child is well but one dye. Your sister is well and her 3 child. John Kittell, your wife and all your child is all well, and all them prisoners taken at Nashaway is all well.

Mr. Rowlandson, se your loving sister his hand C Hanah.

And old Kettel wif his hand.

Brother Rowlandson, pray send thre pound of Tobacco for me, if you can my loving husband pray send thre pound of tobacco for me.

This writing by your enemies—Samuel Uskattuhgun and Gunrashit, two Indian sagamores."

John Hoar was then consulted and it was decided to send Peter Tatatiquinea, alias Conway, with Nepanet with a second request, the copy of which has never been unearthed. Their arrival in Camp is recorded by Mrs. Rowlandson, who wrote: "Then came Tom and Peter with the second letter from the council, about the captives. Though they were Indians I gat them by the hand, and burst out into tears; my heart was so full that I could not speak to them; but recovering myself, I asked them how my husband did? and all my friends and acquaintance? they said they were well, but very melancholy. . . . When the letter was come, the Saggamores met to consult about the captives, and called me to them, to enquire how much my husband would give to redeem me: When I came I sat down among them, as I was wont to do, as their manner is: Then they bid me stand up, and said they were the general court. They bid me speak what I thought he would give. Now knowing that all that we had was destroyed by the Indians, I was in a great strait. I thought if I should speak of but a little, it would be slighted, and hinder the matter; if of a great sum, I knew not where it would be procured; yet at a venture, I said twenty pounds, yet desired them to take less; but they would not hear of that, but sent the message to Boston, that for twenty pounds I should be redeemed. It was a praying Indian that wrote their letters for them. There was another praying Indian, who told me that he had a brother, that would not eat horse, his conscience was so tender and scrupulous, though as large as hell for the destruction of poor christians." A part of the Scriptures was read to the brother, referring to a famine in Samaria, and the sale of an ass's head to be used as food. "He expounded this place to his brother, and shewed him that it was lawful to eat that in a famine, which it is not at another time. And now says he, he will eat horse with any Indian of them all."

The reply to this second letter was discovered. It was written by the well-known Indian, James Printer, who as a child had attended the Indian Charity School at Harvard, who later served many years in the printing office of Samuel Green in Cambridge, and who also greatly assisted John Eliot with his Indian Bible. This note was addressed "for the Governor and the Council at Boston" and read:

"The Indians, Tom Nepennomp and Peter Tatatiquinea hath brought us letter from you about the English Captives, especially for Mrs. Rolanson; the answer is I am sorrow that I haue don much wrong to you, for when we began quarrel at first with Plimouth men I did not think that you should haue so much truble as now is: therefore I am willing to hear your desire about the Captives. Therefore we desire you to sent Mr. Rolanson and goodman Kettel: (for their wives) and these Indians Tom and Peter to redeem their wives, they shall come and goe very safely: Whereupon we ask Mrs. Rolanson, how much your husband willing to giue for you she gaue an answer 20 pound in goodes but John Kittels wife could not till. and the rest captives may be spoken of hereafter."

The Twentieth "Remove" was only a short distance to a place where the Indians built a great wigwam and made preparations for a big dance. Presently John Hoar, the friend of the Indian, with the same two messengers, appeared in camp one Sunday morning. Upon seeing the Englishman approach on horseback, the Indians began to shoot over, under and ahead of his horse, merely to show him what they could do. Hoar and his small delegation brought with them a third letter, the twenty pounds ransom in money and goods, and a pound of tobacco for Mrs. Rowlandson from her husband which she sold for nine shillings. She begged to be allowed to see Mr. Hoar, and was later permitted to do so. "In the morning Mr. Hoar invited the Saggamores to dinner; but when we went to get it ready, we found they had stolen the greatest part of the provisions Mr. Hoar had brought. And we may see the wonderful power of God, in that one passage, in that when there was such a number of them together, and so greedy of a little good food, and no English there but Mr. Hoar and myself, that there they did not knock us on the head, and take what we had; there being not only some provision, but also trading cloth, a part of the 20 pounds agreed upon: But instead of doing us any mischief, they seemed to be ashamed of the fact. . . . Mr. Hoar called them betime to dinner, but they eat but little, they being so busy in dressing themselves and getting ready for their dance: which was carried on by eight of them, four men and four Squaws; my master and mistress being two. He was dressed in his Holland shirt, with great stockings, his garters hung round with shillings, and had girdles of wampom upon his head and shoulders."

Then follows her description of Weetamoe, Quinnapin's wife (quoted elsewhere). The captive woman then continues in her memoirs: "When we were lain down, my master went out of the wigwam, and by and by sent in an Indian called James the Printer, who told Mr. Hoar, that my master would let me go home to-morrow, if he would let him have one pint of liquor. Then Mr. Hoar called his own Indians, Tom and Peter, and bid them all go and see if he would promise it before them three; and if he would he should have it, which he did and had it. Philip smelling the business, called me to him, and asked me what I would give him, to tell me some good news, and to speak a good word for me, that I might go home tomorrow? I told him I could not tell what to give him, I would any thing I had, and asked him what he would have? He said two coats, and 20 shillings in money, half a bushel of seed corn, and some tobacco. I thanked

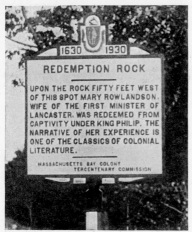

From "Historical Markers, erected by Massachusetts Bay Colony Tercentenary Commission"
Kindness of Hon. Frederic W. Cook, Secretary of the Commonwealth of Massachusetts

REDEMPTION ROCK, PRINCETON, MASSACHUSETTS

Where Mary Rowlandson, wife of the first minister of Lancaster, Massachusetts, was redeemed from captivity under King Philip in the year 1676. During the Indian raid on Lancaster, she was captured and purchased by one of Philip's leading warriors, Quinnapin, who was married to Weetamoe, a sister of the wife of Philip. The account of her captivity and "removes" has come down to us in book form and is most interesting and vivid. The words recorded on a tablet on the rock are: "Upon this rock May 2nd, 1676, was made the agreement for the ransom of Mrs. Mary Rowlandson of Lancaster between the Indians and John Hoar of Concord." King Philip was with the Indians, but refused his consent.

him for his love, but I knew that good news as well as that crafty fox."

After much haranguing a General Court was called and the Indians, with the exception of Philip, voted to let her go home. Her release was obtained on May 2nd and she proceeded in company with Mr. Hoar and the two Indian messengers to her old town of Lancaster, where not a single house remained standing and not a white man was to be seen. They continued to Boston, where the weary wife met her husband after an absence of eleven weeks and five days. While here she learned that the twenty pounds of ransom money had been raised by some women of Boston and by a Mr. Usher. Thomas Shepard, minister of Charlestown, received them into his house, where they resided for eleven weeks. Shortly after this, her sister was redeemed. As Mr. and Mrs. Rowlandson were riding between Ipswich and Rowley, they learned that their son, Joseph, and their nephew were at Portsmouth, and that their daughter had escaped and was then in Providence, under the care of the Governor of Rhode Island. In a few days the family, after their terrible experiences, were again united at Dorchester, where "the South Church in Boston hired an house for us." They then removed to Boston to the house of a friend, James Whitcomb, where they resided until May, 1677, beginning housekeeping again within bare walls. They were assisted by friends here and in England—"Instead of husks we now have the fat calf," she wrote.

The downfall of King Philip was near at hand, and it seems apparent that the disagreement between him and the other chiefs over the question of Mrs. Rowlandson's ransom and release finally led to a rupture between the Pokanokets and Narragansetts. King Philip was so disgusted that he and a number of his warriors separated from the Nipmucks and other Indians in the interior and departed for their own country, where later on they were more easily subdued.

From a photograph   *Kindness of the Bourne Historical Society and the late Percival H. Lombard*

REPRODUCTION OF THE APTUCXET TRADING POST, AT MANAMET, NOW
BOURNE, CAPE COD, MASSACHUSETTS

The original building, erected on this same spot in 1627, was the first trading station to be established by the Plymouth Colony, and played a vital part in the financial struggles of the early settlers and the Indians. It was here that wampum, or Indian money, was first introduced to the colonists as legal tender by the Dutch, and in its manufacture the Indians were very skillful. This station and its stock of goods were specifically named in the first business contract written and signed in America—a three-party agreement between the Colony, Governor Bradford, and the men in London who had financed the expedition. Governor Bradford and others agreed to hold the monopoly of the trade for a term of six years. Many Indian and Dutch implements and utensils were unearthed here, and were on exhibition for some time in the banking rooms of the State Street Trust Company.

APTUCXET TRADING POST, THE "CRADLE OF AMERICAN COMMERCE"

Aptucxet, an Indian name meaning "at the little trap river," was the first trading post established by the Plymouth Colony and played a most vital part in the financial struggles of both the Indians and the early settlers. Here the former brought skins and furs for "trucke," as they expressed it, meaning exchange; here the Dutch from New Amsterdam used to convey sugar, tobacco, cloth and material from Holland to trade with the Plymouth Colonists; here the English by way of the Scusset River on the north side of the Cape conveyed their goods to what is now Sagamore, thence by portage to this trading post to "avoyd the compasing of Cap-Codd, and those deangerous shoulds; and so make any vioage to ye southward in much shorter time, and with farr less danger," as Governor Bradford explains; and for this purpose a "smale pinass" (pinnace) was built at Aptucxet to assist in the transport of their goods.

The original trading post was erected in 1627 "that they might ye better take all convenient opportunitie to follow their trade, both to maintaine themselves, and to disingage them of those great sumes which they stood charged with, and bound for"; it was also built "for

ye saftie of their vessell & goods," as this same authority puts it.
Here they kept some servants, who planted corn and reared some
swine, "and were allwayes ready to goe out with ye barke when there
was occasion. All which tooke good effecte, and turned to their
profite."

One of the most interesting events in the annals of this trading house
was the introduction there of wampumpeag, or Indian money, as early
as October of the year 1627, a few months after the establishment of
the post: This information comes from a report in the National
Archives at The Hague, in which it is set down that the West Indian
Company through its representative, Isaac de Rasiere, then Secretary
at New Amsterdam, had been the person to show it to the colonists.
This form of money was employed by the English and the Indians
as "legal tender" until 1661, but it was used in trade for a number of
years afterwards throughout the Colonies. This introduction of
wampum was "an event of much historical interest as it marks a pre-
liminary step in the development of our currency," explained the late
Percival H. Lombard, at the time President of the Bourne Historical
Society and prime mover in the recent restoration of the trading post.

This important incident was referred to by Governor Bradford in
his history under the year 1628: "But that which turned most of their
profite, in time, was an entrance into the trade of Wampampeake; for
they now bought about 50 li. (probably meaning fathoms) worth of
it of them; any they tould them how vendable it was at their Forte
Orania (now Albany); and did perswade them they would find it so
at Kenebeck; and so it came to pass, in time, though at first it stuck,

From Mrs. Martha J. Lamb's "History of the City of New York"   *Kindness of the late Percival H. Lombard*

TRADING WITH THE INDIANS

& it was 2 years before they could put of this small quantity, till ye inland people knew of it; and afterwards they could scarce ever gett enough for them for many years togeather. And so this with their other provissions, cutt of ther trade quite from ye fishermen, and in great part from other of ye stragling planters. And strange it was to see the great allteration it made, in a few years amonge ye Indeans them selves; for all the Indeans of these parts, & ye Massachusetts, had none or very little of it, but ye sachems and some spetiall persons that wore a litle of it, for ornamente. Only it was made and kepte a m o n g e ye Nariganssets and Pequents (Pequots), which grew

Kindness of the late Percival H. Lombard

LEAD TAG FOR MARKING FURS FOUND WITHIN THE FOUNDATIONS OF THE APTUCXET TRADING POST IN 1930, AND NOW IN THE COLLECTION PRESERVED IN THE BUILDING

Many other articles were found in the vicinity, including war paint, arrow and spear heads, tools for dressing skins, sinkers for fishnets, and other items of interest.

From a photograph. Kindness of C. C. Willoughby, Curator Emeritus of the Peabody Museum, and Donald Scott. Director, Peabody Museum of Archæology and Ethnology, Cambridge, Massachusetts

WAMPUM BELTS IN THE PEABODY MUSEUM OF HARVARD UNIVERSITY

The white shells corresponded to our silver and the black to our gold. The former money was made from the stems of the periwinkle shell and from the white part of the quahaug shell. The latter was made from the dark spot in the quahaug shell. Both, when strung, were known as wampumpeag, commonly known as wampum. The black were twice the value of the white.

rich and potent by it, and these people were pore & begerly, and had no use of it. Neither did the English of this plantation, or any other in ye land, till now that they had knowledg of it from ye Dutch, so much as know what it was, much less that it was a comoditie of that worth & valew. But after it grue thus to be a comoditie in these parts, these Indeans fell into it allso, and to learne how to make it; for ye Narigansets doe geather ye shells of which they make it, from their shors. And it hath now continued a current comoditie aboute this 20 years, and it may prove a drugg in time. In ye mean time it makes ye Indeans of these parts rich and power full and also prowed therby; and fills them with peeces, powder, and shote, which no laws can restraine, by reasone of ye bassnes of sundry unworthy persons, both English, Dutch and French, which may turne to ye ruine of many."

This form of legal tender was first made by the Narragansetts and then by the Pequots, both sometimes called "mint-masters"

From "A Popular History of the United States," by Bryant and Gay   *Permission of Charles Scribner's Sons*

TRADING FOR FURS

for this reason, and was brought here by the Dutch, who realized its value and convenience as a medium of exchange. The Indians became very skilled in its manufacture and no white man was able to make it. Wampum was manufactured from shells. There were two denominations, white and black, the former corresponding to our silver and the latter to our gold. The former was made from the stems or inner whorls of the shell of the periwinkle and also from the white part of the quahaug shell, called "Venus Mercenaria," which is quite common along the southern coast of New England and on Long Island. The latter denomination was made from the dark spot in the quahaug shell, and was of twice the value of the white money, of which six pieces were equivalent to one penny in English currency. When strung, the beads were called wampumpeag, the last syllable "peag" meaning "strung beads."

It may be of interest to mention that the Dutch name for wampumpeag was "Seewan," and large quantities of it were obtained from a place on the eastern end of Long Island known now as Sewanika, from which word comes the name Seawanhaka. Large quantities of quahaug shells must have been used in trade at Falmouth, only a few miles from the Post, for the Indian name for this town was "Succannusset," signifying "the place where the shell money is made." Mr. Lombard, in writing to the Trust Company of its manufacture and usages, said: "The exact process of making the beads is not known, although it is certain that to bore the beads with a stone drill was the work of deft artisans who must then polish them on stones in a weary round of labor, for all accounts agree that the finished product had a

certain elegance of its own. In the shell heaps of New England are hidden the old flint awls of prehistoric design which may have been spun by a small bow such as jewelers employ at present. One end of the stick into which the drill was placed was held against the thigh and made to rotate continually by means of the bow while holding the bit of shell against the drill. The beads were strung on fibres of hemp or the tendons taken from the flesh of wild animals. Wampumpeag was usually measured in fathoms, or 6 feet, the Dutch unit of trade. When 6 white beads passed for a penny the fathom was 360 beads, but if it were 4, as under the Massachusetts standard of 1640, then the fathom was 240 beads. Thus the fathom became the name for a count, an enumeration, rather than a unit of length."

"Besides using wampumpeag for coinage and for personal adornment, it was extensively employed in treaties. The belts were made use of not only in connection with treaties, but were employed for other rites and ceremonies. Each bead, its color, size and location had its special significance. When strings of 'peag' were embroidered on strips of deer skin they became 'Machequoce,' girdles or belts. A very fine specimen of a treaty belt is in the collection of the Peabody Museum at Cambridge, shown in an illustration. The name and general use of wampum are familiar enough, but the volume, importance and effect of it upon trade have been forgotten. Its intrinsic value was derived from the fact that strings of shells were by the Indians highly esteemed as ornaments and could always be turned to good account in that way when their owner had no immediate use for them in trade. They were ornaments first and became a monetary currency because of their convenience and universal acceptability. For this

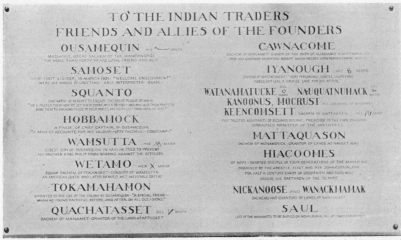

From a photograph   Kindness of the late Percival H. Lombard

INDIAN TRADERS' TABLET IN APTUCXET TRADING POST AT MANAMET, NOW BOURNE, MASSACHUSETTS

Set up in memory of the Indian friends and allies who lived in the territory served by the post. Ousamequin (Massasoit), Samoset, Squanto, Hobomok, Wamsutta, Weetamoe and Tokamahamon are mentioned elsewhere in these pages.

Reproduced by permission of the Governor and Committee of the   *Kindness of the late Percival H. Lombard*
Hudson's Bay Company

THE FIRST SALE OF FURS AT GARRAWAY'S COFFEE HOUSE, LONDON, 1671

Most of the furs sent to London from New England came from the Kennebec Post, in Maine, but other furs were shipped there from the Bourne Post.

reason the Dutch at Manhattan were quick to see their value in barter."

It is probable that certain persons were authorized to make this Indian money and it is also probable that there was some system of detecting its genuineness from the way it was made; for later on, when it was counterfeited to a large extent, the Indians became very expert in picking out the genuine from the bad. Roger Williams noted that the Indian merchants were "marvelous subtle in their bargains. Therefore they will beat all markets and try all places, and run twenty— thirty, yea forty miles and more to save expense. They are as full of business and as impatient of hindrance as any merchant in Europe."

Illustrations appear in the text showing the Indian Traders' Tablet set up in the Trading Post, together with other items of interest.

Those interested in our commerce will be surprised to learn that this Aptucxet Trading Post was especially referred to in the first business contract actually written and signed in America. Up to that time, the year 1626, all agreements relating to explorations, colonization and fishing expeditions had been drawn abroad. This contract, therefore, which Governor Bradford quotes in his Letter Book, referring specifically to this Trading Post, "represents the commencement of orderly, well-organized business in this country," as Mr. Lombard expressed it. This little station, now so faithfully reproduced, "assumes a unique

position in our national historic interest," to quote the words of the same writer, and "From it, as one of the very first of the important outposts in New England, and hence in America, has developed the world commerce of the nation. It comes near being the zero mile-stone, if not *the* zero milestone of our commercial progress."

The reproduction of this old Trading Post, with its English, Dutch and Indian relics, should be visited. It is to be found at Bourne, near the western end of the Cape Cod Canal, once the bed of the Manamet River. Here was the beginning of the ancient portage across the isthmus. Manamet, meaning "Trail of the burden carriers," should not be confused with Manomet near Plymouth, or with Monument Beach on Buzzards Bay. (Cape Codders claim that the people of Plymouth stole the name from them, and this is probably true.) The building itself, made possible mainly by the General Society of May-flower Descendants, has been placed on its original foundations, which were discovered in 1852 by Dr. John Bachelder, a resident of Bourne, and William S. Russell, Register of Deeds at Plymouth. The build-ing is surrounded by a twelve-acre park, which includes the original spring and also some plainly visible portions of the old Manamet Portage Path as it starts out across the Cape. During the work of excavation many relics of the early colonial days were unearthed, including Dutch pottery, a key and part of a lock, a candle-stick, pipes,

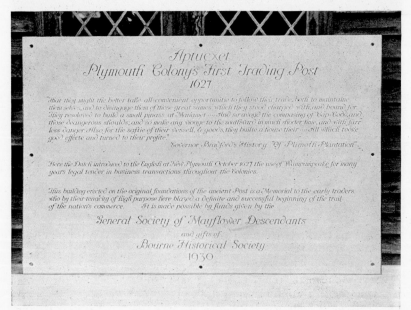

From a photograph   *Kindness of the Bourne Historical Society and the late Percival H. Lombard*

APTUCXET TRADING POST TABLET

Recording the reason for the placing here of this first trading post of the Plymouth Colony, as explained by Governor Bradford. This tablet also notes the introduction of wampumpeag to the colonists. The building was dedicated on September 3, 1930, and was made possible by the General Society of Mayflower Descendants, the Bourne Historical Society, the New England Society in the City of New York, and many individual citizens who contributed to the purchase of the surround-ing land and provided an endowment fund which is in the care of the State Street Trust Company.

buckles, a hoe, spurs and horse's bit, trading knives, a trinket, lead tag for attaching to furs, and stone implements. This collection was on exhibition a few years ago in the banking rooms of the State Street Trust Company, which also acted as depository of the restoration fund that was raised. An interesting relic is the ancient stone doorstep of the First Indian Mission Church at Cumassakumkanet, now Bournedale, a picture of which will be used in a later brochure. All of the stepping stones at the entrance are the originals, and some of the old bricks may be seen in the large fireplace and chimney.

This building, shown in an illustration, serves, to quote Mr. Lombard again, as a "memorial to the early traders who, by their tenacity of high purpose, blazed a definite and successful beginning of the trail of the nation's commerce."

Before closing these chapters, we believe it will be of interest to quote from an excellent speech of the Honorable Edward Everett. He was speaking of this great continent before the Pilgrims came, and of the situation of its primitive inhabitants. "I saw one or two of them, poor wanderers, as we came into Plymouth, seated by the roadside, wondering spectators of the pageant which was passing before their eyes.

"A few days ago, as I saw in the newspapers, two light, birch-bark canoes appeared in Boston harbor, containing each a solitary Indian. They seemed, as they approached, to gaze in silent wonder at the city of the triple hills, rising street above street, and crowned with the dome of the State House, and at the long line of villas stretching far into the back-ground; at the numerous tall vessels, outward bound, as they dropped down the channel, and spread their broad wings to the breeze, and those which were returning, weather-beaten, from the ends of the earth; at the steamers, dashing in every direction across the harbor, breathing volumes of smoke from their fiery lungs. They paddled their frail barks with dexterity and speed through this strange, busy and to them, no doubt, bewildering scene; and, having made the circuit of East Boston, the Navy Yard, the city itself and South Boston, dropped down with the current, and disappeared among the islands.

"There was not a human being of kindred blood to utter a word of welcome to them, in all the region, which, on the day we now commemorate (August 1st, 1620) was occupied by their forefathers in Massachusetts. The race is gone."

Francis Parkman, referring to the same subject says: "The Indian is a true child of the forest and the desert. The wastes and solitudes of nature are his congenial home. His haughty mind is imbued with the spirit of the wilderness, and the light of civilization falls on him with a blighting power. His unruly pride and untamed freedom are in harmony with the lonely mountains, cataracts and rivers among which he dwells; and primitive America, with her savage scenery and savage men, opens to the imagination a boundless world, unmatched in wild sublimity."